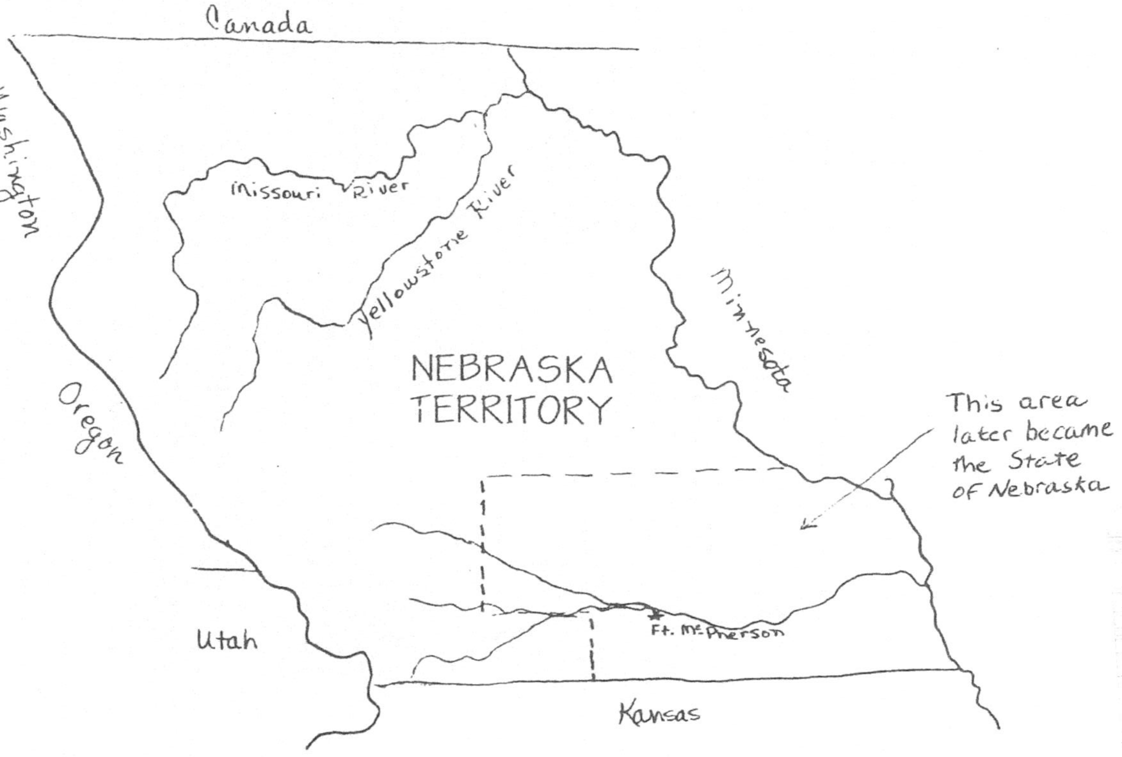

Original Territory of Nebraska

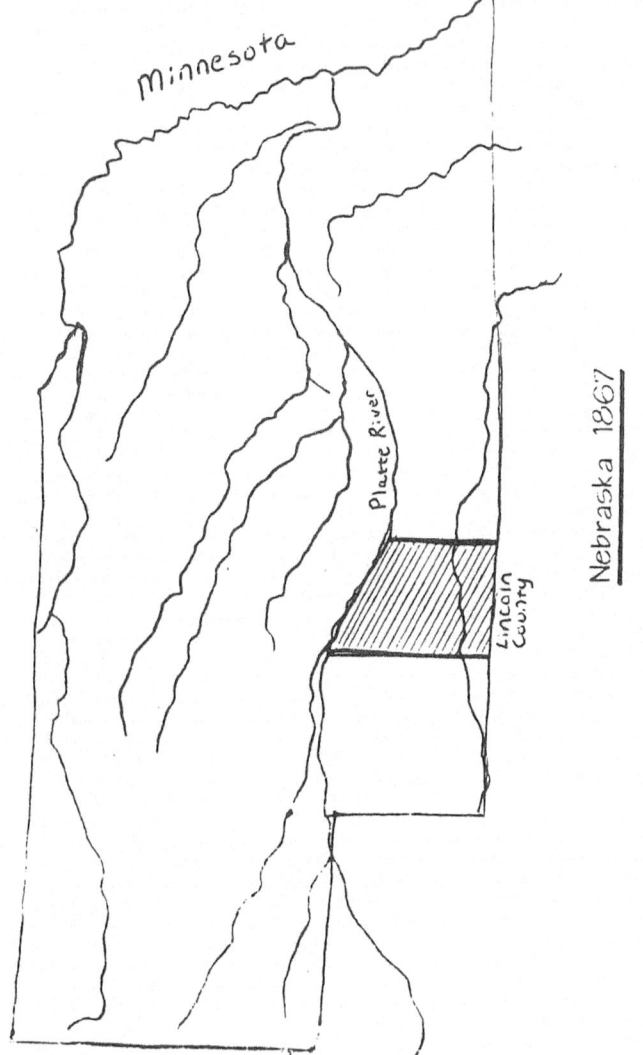

PRE-STATEHOOD HISTORY
OF
LINCOLN COUNTY, NEBRASKA

Ruby Roberts Coleman

Prepared for
Nebraska's 125th Anniversary Commission
Quasquicentennial, 1867–1992
on Behalf of
Sioux Lookout Chapter D.A.R.

HERITAGE BOOKS
2025

HERITAGE BOOKS
AN IMPRINT OF HERITAGE BOOKS, INC.

Books, CDs, and more—Worldwide

For our listing of thousands of titles see our website
at
www.HeritageBooks.com

A Facsimile Reprint
Published 2025 by
HERITAGE BOOKS, INC.
Publishing Division
5810 Ruatan Street
Berwyn Heights, MD 20740

Copyright © 1992 Ruby Roberts Coleman

— Publisher's Notice —
In reprints such as this, it is often not possible to remove blemishes from the original. We feel the contents of this book warrant its reissue despite these blemishes and hope you will agree and read it with pleasure.

International Standard Book Number
Paperbound: 978-1-55613-613-9

TABLE OF CONTENTS

FOREWORD v

CHAPTER 1
THE LAND, THE RIVER ... AND THE WIND 1

CHAPTER 2
EARLY EXPLORERS AND TRAVELERS 5

CHAPTER 3
CIVILIZATION IN WESTWARD MOTION 15

CHAPTER 4
OLD SHORTER COUNTY 25

CHAPTER 5
PLATTE VALLEY CHARACTERS 39

CHAPTER 6
MESSRS. PALLERDY AND MORIN 53

CHAPTER 7
MILITARY ALONG THE PLATTE VALLEY 59

CHAPTER 8
RAILS TO NORTH PLATTE 79

ADDENDUM 1
  SHORTER COUNTY, NEBRASKA TERRITORY
  1860 Nebraska Territorial Census &
  Mortality Schedule 89

ADDENDUM 2
  PRE-STATEHOOD MARRIAGES OF
  SHORTER/LINCOLN COUNTY, NEBRASKA
  TERRITORY 97

ADDENDUM 3
  COMMANDING OFFICERS OF FORT
  COTTONWOOD/FORT MCPHERSON 103

ADDENDUM 4
  COUNTY COMMISSIONER RECORDS
  LINCOLN COUNTY, NEBRASKA
  October, 1866 107

ADDENDUM 5
  PENISTON & MILLER ACCOUNT LEDGER
  January 1, 1867 - February 29, 1867 111

ADDENDUM 6
  PRE-STATEHOOD TOWNS AND VILLAGES
  OF LINCOLN COUNTY, NEBRASKA 123

BIBLIOGRAPHY 127

INDEX i

FOREWORD

On behalf of the Sioux Lookout Chapter, D.A.R., this book has been prepared for the Nebraska's 125th Anniversary Commission Quasquicentennial 1867-1992.

History of the county did not begin with statehood on March 1, 1867. It began much earlier.

Those who passed through here and those who stayed before that date were responsible for shaping and molding the county. This is a history of those early explorations and settlements in what would become Shorter County and then Lincoln County, all before Nebraska became a state.

The county was settled from east to west, along a path formed by nature. It was a path long in use, from the days of the mighty herds of buffalo to the warring tribes of Native American Indians. The path followed a river, not as large as some on the continent, but unusual and worthy in its own right. It was only natural that the first explorers, traders, trappers and adventurers would follow that well-used path.

With some understanding of the early beginnings of the county, I feel that the achievement of statehood can be better appreciated.

Ruby Roberts Coleman

CHAPTER 1

THE LAND, THE RIVER ... AND THE WIND

Touched, caressed, then ravaged and abused by the wind, the unnamed land survived. The land was yet to be known by man. In its youth the land was soft, rippling sand, tossed and swirled by the wind. As it grew older the grasses would tease and torment its surface and flutter in the wind. Coursing across the land was a river. Its water was flat and wide and most of the time not very swift. As it flowed toward the east, the wind splashed the water onto the shallow banks, forming mounds of sand, creating new plateaus and sandbars on the land. And always there was the wind.

This expanse of land would eventually be known as Nebraska and a particular part of that land would be known as Lincoln County. All this would take time.

Standing erect and tall, hair blowing in the wind, skin burnished by the sun, prehistoric man trod the land. The land and the river were not alone. Dipping his hands into the water and digging his toes deep into the sand, man made his mark upon the land.

In our part of the land as yet unofficially named, the historic tribes of the Pawnee, the Arapaho and the Cheyenne began to roam. The Pawnee may have moved into the valleys of the river from the south and southwest. They were probably in the area as early as 1541 when Francisco Vasquez de Coronado explored the plains in search of the legendary cities of gold.

The Arapaho and Cheyenne, the sedentary Siouan tribes, were in the area as early as 1800 when they were raiding and hunting.

The river flowing through the land was called the *Nibathaska* or *Nibrathka* by the Indians. To the Pawnee it was known as the *Kizkatuz* which meant flat or shallow and some called it the *Kisparuksti* which meant wonderful river. It provided sustenance also for countless herds of bison and eventually the land became scarred with their trails. From the forks of the north and south river eastward were numerous camps of the Pawnee Indians. Those living along the river were the *Chau-i* (Grand) group. The early French traders knew them as *Grand Pani*.

The Pawnee greatly respected the river and land as evidenced from their song ...

> *Behold on Mother Earth the running streams!*
> *Behold the promise of her fruitfulness!*
> *Truly her power gives she us.*
> *Give thanks to Mother Earth who lieth here.*

CHAPTER 2

EARLY EXPLORERS AND TRAVELERS

In 1714 the French explorer, Etienne Veniard de Bourgmond, ascended the Missouri River to the mouth of the Platte. He called the river the *Nebraska* or flat water. This was the first time that word had appeared in writing.

The river and the land would be known by various names. Eventually it would be called the *Platte River*, meaning flat, by white explorers. Some would refer to it as the *Moonshell* which was a poetic Indian name. To anyone viewing it, the river would appear unuseable, unnavigable and of little consequence. Yet the Platte would become an important water-course by creating a natural corridor for the migration of civilization westward from the Mississippi.

In 1720, Don Pedro de Villasur, commanding a force of 45 Spanish soldiers, 60 Indian allies, a priest and interpreter, left Santa Fe for a reconnaissance with the French on the Great Plains. In June of that year they journeyed by way of Taos toward French towns which had been established in the area of the *Rio de Jesus y Maria*. This was a name given the South Platte River by the Indian scout, Jose Naranjo, in the company of Villasur.

Upon reaching the river, this inadequate yet courageous force had not enountered the French. Therefore, they assumed Spain's sovereignty over the area. On August 12, 1720, Villasur's forces camped on the south bank of the Platte River opposite a Pawnee village. The next morning they prepared to depart for Santa Fe. That night, Pawnees under French influence, crossed the Platte River and early on the morning of August 13th attacked the Spanish troops.

Forty-four members of the troop, including Villasur, were killed. The Franciscan priest, Father Juan Minguez, and the interpreter, Juan de l'Archeveque, were also killed. Ironically, de l'Archeveque had been a companion to La Salle who had explored and conquered the Mississippi Valley in the name of France.

While some researchers feel that this incident took place in the eastern portion of what would become the state of Nebraska, still others feel that it occurred slightly east and south of the present city of North Platte in Lincoln County. This would place the incident south of the South Platte River.

In June of 1739, Paul and Pierre Mallett explored the valley of the Platte River in an attempt to find an overland route to Santa Fe. These two French-Canadians along with six of their friends came south and west through the Great Lakes area, down the Illinois and up the Mississippi River to the Missouri River.

They had mistakenly been informed that Santa Fe was to be found at the headwaters of the Missouri River. Their log pirogues only took them further north. Eventually they found a small river (now known as the Niobrara) flowing into the Missouri. At this point they decided to abandon the river and journey southward across the plains.

The Mallets and their friends found a Pawnee Indian camp and soon discovered that the Indians understood their French. With some bartering they obtained horses and with the Indian chief's directions they headed southwest. The flowing sands and rippling grasses of the prairie became the voyageurs' river.

On June 2, 1739 they reached a flat river which they named *La Riviere Plate*. They came as far west as the forks of the North Platte and South Platte River, approximately three miles east of the present city of North Platte. Continuing their quest for a route to Santa Fe, this small group eventually reached Spanish territory. By following the area rivers and streams southward they reached Taos on July 15, 1739. One week later they reached Santa Fe.

The river they christened La Platte would retain that nomenclature throughout the centuries.

In 1762 the brothers Pierre and Auguste Choteau were sent out from St. Louis to explore the Northwest with the thought of establishing trading posts for the purpose of securing furs from the Indians. Little is known of their expedition except that they did pass up the Platte River beyond the forks of the north and south tributaries. For several years this type of exploration continued from St. Louis. In 1780 an expedition was sent to explore the area between the Missouri River and the Rocky Mountains. They traversed to the area now known as Yellowstone and thence down into the area of the North Platte river. In about 1784 or 1785 they were in the area of what is now North Platte and crossed the Platte River near Willow Island in what is now Dawson County. The result of this type of exploration resulted in the establishment of a few trading post and trade with the Indians.

In 1803 the land which would be named Nebraska became a part of the United States, as a result of the Louisiana Purchase. On April 30, 1803 France ceded the western half of the Mississippi Valley to the United States. This was comprised of 828,000 square miles or over 500 million acres. This acquisition was approved by the Senate on October 20, 1803 and the United States took formal possession on December 20, 1803.

On August 31, 1803 Capt. Meriwether Lewis (President Jefferson's Secretary) and William Clark began exploration of the lands west of the Mississippi. They traveled 8,000 miles via the Ohio, Missouri and Columbia rivers to the Pacific Ocean with a similar return route. Their expedition ended on September 23, 1806 at St. Louis. While they did not pass through the area which would later become Lincoln County, their exploration opened the way for future parties to explore and later inhabit the area. A map of 1802 showed this area as Lousiane with the Plate river drawn in along with a large island just east of the forks of the river.

In 1812 Robert Stuart and six others employed by John Jacob Astor reached Court House Rock in the middle of the winter. In the spring of 1813, they arrived at the Missouri River and became the first white men to traverse what became known as the Great Platte River Road. Their route most likely took them through what would eventually become Lincoln County.

In 1819 Major Stephen H. Long followed the Platte and South Platte Rivers through Nebraska. His expedition was the first to specifically gather scientific information on the area. Major Long was an engineer and in his group were a botanist, geologist, zoologist, assistant naturalist, landscape painter and two topographical engineers along with soldiers and packers. A total of 20 white men were in the group.

On June 6, 1819 the Long expedition broke up their camp on the banks of the Missouri River and began their exploration to find the sources of the Platte River in the Rocky Mountains. Their trek led them along the north side of the Platte River to the forks of the North Platte and South Platte east of the present city of North Platte. At that point they crossed both of the rivers and proceeded up the south bank of the South Platte. Their route took them over the area now included in the present city of North Platte. They crossed from Nebraska into Colorado not far from the present city of Julesburg, Colorado on June 21, 1819.

While they failed to find the head waters of the Platte River, they did discover the mountain now known as Long's Peak, in Colorado. Members of the party were also the first to climb to the top of Pike's Peak. The expedition returned eastward to the Mississippi River trailing the Arkansas River.

Long's expedition reported that the region over which they had passed was unfit for agriculture and detailed it on their maps as the "Great Desert." Long reported the following about the land now known as Lincoln County: "The bottom lands of the river rise by an imperceptible ascent on each side, extending laterally to a distance of from two to ten miles, where they are terminated by low ranges of gravelly hills, running parallel to the general direction of the river. Beyond these the surface is an undulating plain, having an elevation of from fifty to one hundred feet, and presenting the aspect of hopeless and irreclaimable sterility."

The report of the expedition was widely circulated both on this continent and in Europe. It would take others with greater foresight to break ground and settle the area, realizing its true value and worth.

Thomas Fitzpatrick and James Clyman followed the Platte River from the mountains to the Missouri River in the spring of 1824. Their group also included Edward Rose, Louis Vasquez, Jim Bridger, David E. Jackson, Hugh Glass, Seth Grant and Jedediah Smith. They most likely came through this area.

In 1825, William Ashley, a soldier and fur trader from St. Louis spent a part of the winter at the forks on the Platte River. There he found a band of Pawnee Indians under the leadership of Chief Two Ax. In January the chief and his tribe furnished Ashley and his men with a buffalo surround. Possibly because of the information passed on by Ashley, the first wagon train left St. Louis in 1830 and passed through what would later become Lincoln County. Ashley's exploration of the area resulted in the opening of a new route and trade area and the advent of the summer rendezvous which brought traders, trappers and Indians together.

The Smith-Jackson-Sublette partnership led a caravan from St. Louis, Missouri to the Wind River rendezvous in 1830. Theirs was the first wagon train up the Platte River, passing through this area. Their train was comprised of 10 wagons drawn by 4 mules each, 2 Dearborns drawn by 1 mule each and 81 men mounted on mules. They reported about the feasibility of their route to John Eaton, Secretary of War.

In 1835, Col. Henry Dodge, visited the area while in the employment of the United States Government. His expedition consisted of 117 men and was for the purpose of inducing the Arickaree Indians to abandon their wild life and become civilized. The government in exchange would provide aid for them. This expedition camped at what would later be called Cottonwood Springs. At that place they endeavoured to hold a council with the Indians. The Indians, however, fled to the head of Fremont Slough in the nearby area. On July 5, 1835, Dodge was successful in holding a meeting with them. This took place about ten miles southwest of the present city of North Platte. The result of the meeting was a promise of good will and friendship on the part of the Indians, reciprocated by presents from the whites.

In 1842 John Fremont traveled through the country. At that time he found some trappers located about 15 miles east of the forks of the Platte River on an island. The leader of this group of trappers was a man named Brady, so Fremont named the island Brady's Island and marked it as such on his map. It is thought that Brady was killed by Indians in about 1859.

There is still another version of the naming of the island. In 1833 a party was descending the Platte River using boats of hides stretched over pole frames and tarred at the seams. They were taking beaver skins to market and camped on an island below the junction of the two forks of the Platte. One of the men in the group was a man named Brady. He quarreled with a Frenchman in the group. Members of the party returning from a hunt found Brady dead. The Frenchman reported that Brady's death was caused by the accidental discharge of his weapon.

Further down the river the water became very shallow so they abandoned their boats. Dividing their packs the Frenchman took the portion which had belonged to Brady. The next evening, when he was trying to light his fire by the discharge of his pistol he supposedly shot himself in the thigh. Since he was isolated from the rest of the group it was six days before he was found by Pawnee Indians. The Frenchman died a few days later, but confessed before his death to the murder of Brady.

Fremont and his men celebrated July 4th of that year in what is now Lincoln County. Reportedly the weather was damp and murky and the group proceeded to celebrate the anniversary of the country in a fitting manner. Their camp for that particular day was reportedly west of the present city of North Platte at a place later to be called O'Fallons.

The first missionary came through the area in 1834. In 1836 Narcissa Whitman and Elizabeth or Eliza Spalding were the first white women to journey the valley of the Platte River. The women traveled with their husbands, the missionary doctor Marcus Whitman and the Reverend Henry Harmon Spalding. The Whitman-Satterlee party left Pittsburgh, March 15, 1836. Narcissa Whitman kept written accounts in the form of letters to her mother and often they took on the structure of diary entries. She was fully aware that her journey was unheard of for females. Men who had explored the western regions reported that females would be prevailed upon by the tribes of Indians in a manner of unrestrained passion and also that the fatigues of the journey would be devastating.

Through the written accounts left by Narcissa Whitman, we can thoroughly appreciate her exuberant spirit and keen insight. She was experiencing something no other white woman had ever experienced. In her words, "Our manner of living is far preferable to any in the States. I never was so contented and happy before. Neither have I enjoyed such health for years. In the morn as soon as the day breaks, the first that we hear is the word --- arise, arise. ... We encamp in a large ring-- beggage and men, tents and wagons on the outside and all the animals, except the cows (which) are fastened to pickets, within the circle. This arrangement is to accommodate the guard who stands regularly every night and day, also when we are in motion, to protect our animals from the approach of Indians who would steal them ... We are ready to start, usually at six -- travel till eleven, encamp, rest and feed, start again about two --- travel until six or before if we come to a good tavern -- then encamp for the night."

In her joking and laughing manner Narcissa wrote, "Our table is the ground, our table-cloth is an India rubber cloth, used when it rains as a cloak; our dishes are made of tin --- basins for each cups, iron spoons and plates, each of us, and several pans for milk and to put our meat in when we wish to set it upon the table -- each one carries his own knife in a scabbard and it is always ready for use."

The Whitmans and their party arrived in Fort Vancouver on

September 12, 1836. Whitman and his wife established a mission at Waiilatpu, located twenty miles above Fort Walla Walla. They remained there until November 29, 1847 when Whitman, his wife, Narcissa and their two children were killed in an uprising of the Cayuse Indians in the area which became Washington Territory in 1853.

The Platte River, often referred to as "a mile wide and an inch deep" was a well-written subject in the journals of pioneers traversing its bank on their way west. In 1839 Frederick A. Wizlizenus, M.D. wrote, "The Platte has its source on the eastern slopes of the Rocky Mountains, and has two Main branches (North and South), which, on their union, flow in an easterly direction toward the Missouri. A short distance below the meeting point the river divides afresh, and forms a great long island. At this island we reached the Platte. The river, of which we saw but a small part is not broad at this point with sparse borders of cottonwood. The river is a mile or two broad at either side, and bounded by small hills or bluffs. The river is shallow, but .... one may sink in the quicksand. The very valley is covered with pure river sand." This impressive dividing of the rivers which Wizlizenus and others penned is located in Lincoln County.

Dr. Wislizenus continued his 1839 account with "we reached the junction of the north and south arms of the Platte. The bluffs, like wings of a stage, on either side, had now become more interesting. I climbed one of the highest points to enjoy the view.... Arriving at the top I found considerable strong 'Medicine.' Thirty buffalo skulls, adorned with all kinds of gewgaws, lay before me in a magic circle ..."

The Indians of this area led a free, nomadic life as untamed as that of the buffalo who also roamed their land. The Indians did not attack, but were rather attacked themselves by civilization. According to John Charles Fremont the "Indians and buffalo made the poetry and life of the prairie, and our camp was full of their exhilaration." Dr. Wizlizenus, and those before and after him, had invaded the serenity of the Indian's existence. For the most part the Indians of the Platte Valley observed man's advancement through the area and did not attack in full force until about 1864.

CHAPTER 3

CIVILIZATION IN WESTWARD MOTION

Year by year they came, at first a trickle of mankind in makeshift craft trying to ply the shallow waters of the Platte. Then in small groups they came on horseback and some on foot. Each group of explorers, trappers and adventurers made observations of the area, drew pictures and told others about the uninhabitable, unclaimed land lying somewhere between the Mississippi River and the ocean.

The first bona fide emigrant party left Westport Landing in Missouri in 1841, destination Oregon. Between 1840 and 1866 there were 2,500,000 people who traveled the Platte River valley. They carved a wide, deep trail which made a geographical indentation on the land and an historical impact for future generations.

In July of 1845 the phrase, "manifest destiny" appeared in the *United States Magazine and Democratic Review* in an article by John L. O'Sullivan. In his article, O'Sullivan asserted the right of the American people to cover the continent. In this spirit and with the words manifest destiny on their tongues, rivers of mankind trudged across the central part of the United States.

Their highway was a trail, a path created initially by mere footsteps upon the land. To the Indians it became known as *The Great Medicine Road of the Whites.* People going to Oregon called it the *Oregon Trail*. To the Mormons taking the northern route, it became known as the *Mormon Trail*. Those heading for the gold fields of California referred to it as the *California Trail*. Others called it the *Pony Express Route*, the *Council Bluffs Road* or *Fort Laramie Road*. Geographically it was the great corridor formed by the Platte River.

Alongside the constant clatter of the horses hooves, the clanging of the wagon wheels, and the conversations of the emigrants, the river was silent and endless. It was always there and always unpredictable.

They came like an army ... a misshaped group of people with their own reasons and lust for life and adventure. Raymond N. Doetsch in his book *JOURNEY TO THE GREEN AND GOLDEN LANDS*, called them "... rich men, poor men, beggar men, thieves, farmers, lawyers, doctors, merchants, preachers, workmen, Republicans, Whigs, Federalists. Abolitionists, Baptists, Methodists, Transcendentalists, Campbellites, Millerites, Presbyterians, Mormons, white men, black men, yellow men, Germans, Russians, Poles, Chileans, Swiss, Spaniards, sailors, steamboat men, lumbermen, gamblers, the loose, squint-eyed, pockmarked, one-armed, the bearded, the beardless, the mustachioed, side-whiskered, and goateed, singing, cursing, weeping, and laughing in their sleep."

It is estimated that about 85 percent of the emigrants to California in 1849 were men; 10 percent were women and 5 percent were children. Prior to the discovery of gold in California, the thrust of the emigration had been to Oregon. In 1847 about 5,000 people headed to the northwest and only about 1,000 went to California.

Records left at Fort Kearny and Fort Laramie indicate that in 1849 there were approximately 30,000 Argonauts on their way to California. Historians know that 145 journals have survived from that period of migration.

Along with their baggage, much of which was dropped along the way, the pioneers brought their aches, pains, illnesses and diseases. As late as 1860, few wagon trains had a doctor. Cholera, known as the *Terror of the Plains*, left widespread destruction. Few wagon trains escaped its scourge. Thinking they could outrun the disease, many groups traveled day and night.

On his way to the California gold fields in 1849, Joseph Goldborough Bruff kept a journal complete with drawings. These are now at the library at Downey, California. Bruff seemed rather obsessed with the deaths which occurred along the route. There were approximately 1,500 to 2,000 burials in 1849, most the result of Asiatic cholera. This represented a mortality rate of 6 percent.

Bruff noted that near Clay Bluffs to the left of the forks of the Platte, they buried Lemuel Lee of Vandalia, Illinois, who died June 3, 1849 at 4 p.m., age 64. He died of "prostation consequent upon cholera after an illness of two weeks." At the same site they buried Captain Pleasant Gray of Huntsville, Walker County, Texas, who died June 9 of cholera, after being ill three days. "A little further on" and approximately three miles above the ford of the Platte, S.W. Moore died. A day later, he noted four graves close together, one mile above the ford of the South Fork of the Platte. They were C. Taylor who died of cholera and typhus, David Amich from Missouri, Dr. J.T. Boon from Missouri and J. Smither who died of cholera. Directly at the forks of the Platte, Bruff noted that a grave was placed on the divide marking the burial of J.M. McClanahan of Morgan County, Missouri and Daniel

Maloy of Gallatin County, Illinois who died of cholera. One-half day's journey from the North Fork of the Platte, they buried Jno. Waugh of Scott County, Missouri.

Known also as the *Destroyer of the Great Migration*, cholera claimed 1,000 to 2,500 lives in 1850, averaging four graves per mile between St. Joseph, Missouri and Fort Laramie. For the most part, children seemed relatively immune to the disease, but became orphans when their parents fell prey to it. Cholera struck suddenly and after "great agony" the victim died usually within hours. Not all cases were fatal. Doctors accompanying the wagon trains would often recommend a cure in the form of laudunum with pepper, musk, ammonia, camphor and peppermint. Doses were repeated and sometimes accompanied by mustard plasters.

The lack of sufficient wood along the trail made proper coffin burials impossible. The bodies were often rolled or sewed in a blanket and placed in a hole. If a board of any sort was available, it was placed over the body to protect it from the ravages of wild animals. Most sites were never marked as the pioneers felt that would call the Indians' attention to the trail.

Another emigrant death was that of Thomas Vance. According to a journal kept by emigrants accompanying him to Oregon he was buried in 1844 "about ten miles up the north fork of the Platte River, (on) the north side of the river, in the bottom a few rods from the river." Traditionally the Oregon Trail forked to the South Platte River, however it is known that many emigrant groups varied back and forth in their preference of trails. The grave of Thomas Vance was unmarked and is most likely now under the water of the North Platte River. Both the North Platte and South Platte rivers have changed courses through the years.

The Oregon Trail began in Westport, Missouri in 1841 and lasted for over 20 years. Over this thousands of emigrants traveled the 2,000 miles from western Missouri to Oregon and other areas of the Pacific Northwest.

Journals of the Birmingham Emigrating Company were kept by Leander Vaness Loomis. Along with his brothers, Adoniram Judson, Abner and Andrew, Leander joined the Birmingham Emigrating Company which started from Birmingham, Iowa on April 11, 1850 for California. This particular group bought cattle in the Sacramento Valley and marketed them in mining camps. Their trip to California took them through this area. On May 23, 1850 he wrote, "Got a tolerable early start, passed several Beautiful streams, roads quite Bad, very hard on our teams, Pessed a range of bluffs on the South side of the North fork of the Platte, which was covered with cedar trees, the scenery was highly grand and novel, moved to Day about 23 miles and encamped on the north fork of the Platte." The following day he wrote, "Got an early start, travelled up the North fork of Platt, Bottom narrow, roads about half the way good, the balance verry Sandy, hard on our teams..." This would probably refer to the area around the present communities of Paxton or Sutherland.

Edward Everett wrote, "Take the Bible in one hand and your New England civilization in the other and make your mark on that country." Founders and organizers of the Boston-Newton Company did just that. One morning in 1841 four young men were applying for an apprenticeship course at the Petee Iron Works in Newton Upper Falls, Massachusetts. Charles Gould, David Staples and George Winslow were 17 years of age and the fourth, Brackett Lord, was 21. At the end of 1848 they conceived of the idea of a venture to California. In 1849 gold fever was spreading which probably added fuel to their ideas. The idea of a joint stock association was that the group would pool their assets, such as money, equipment, and labor to achieve a common objective. For the Boston-Newton Joint Stock Association members were assessed $300 each, payable in two installments. This would cover their passage to Independence, Missouri by rail and steamer and pay for the equipment involved in their overland journey along with additional supplies sent to San Francisco by ship.

On a cold clear morning in April 1849 they left Boston. Months later they were crossing Nebraska on their way to Fort Laramie. They recorded in their journals that the river bottom was quicksand making it difficult for their mules to travel. The water (in Lincoln County) was from one to three feet in depth. Crossing the South Fork of the Platte River necessitated removing items from their wagon, an all-day job. They passed the division, thus, of the rivers without knowing it. Staples reported that they came to the crossing of the South Fork of the Platte River at "eliven o'clock." They waited an hour and commenced to cross it. They noted that the "Verginia" company were crossing in a government wagon on the opposite side from them.

Perhaps in the vicinity of Lincoln County, they reported that the road was level, dry and smooth. "Winds on June 19th were blowing with great force, driving dry dust and sand, penetrating every crack and crevice about the wagons and causing the pioneers to have sore eyes." The following date they reported violent rain and thunder storms with muddy roads. Their journals relate that the sand bluffs along the Platte River "represented minature mountain scenery, having been worked into a variety of formations from the rain and wind."

In 1850 James W. Evans of another wagon group wrote that "from the sandhills, it (the Platte) had the appearance of a great inland sea. It looked wider than the Mississippi and showed to much better advantage, there being no timber on the banks to check the scope of the human eye. My first impression on beholding the Platte River was, that as it looked so wide and so muddy, and rolled along within three feet of the top of the bank with such majesty that it was unusually swollen and perfectly impassable. Judge my surprise when I learned that it was only 3-4 feet deep. The water is sandy and filled with glittering particles of micah or isingglass that its waves appear to be floating with gold."

Joel Palmer recorded in 1845 that they had crossed the line that separates civilized man from the wilderness. All they did was pass through on their way to the real gold fields of California, the untamed Far West. It would take the Indian scares and skirmishes of the 1860s to eventually settle and tame the area that would become Lincoln County.

The restless population did not cease moving west in 1849. In 1850 approximately 55,000 went to California and in 1852 another 50,000 migrated there. In 1852 approximately 10,000 journeyed to Oregon. This mass migration did not slack until Indian problems occurred in the 1860's. By then 300,000 people had moved west and the United States was connected from sea to shining sea.

In the spring of 1847 an unusual group of pioneers headed west from Winter Quarters at Florence in eastern Nebraska, near Omaha. They had been driven from Missouri to Illinois where they had built a large temple at Nauvoo. From there they were driven across Iowa in search of religious freedom. Over 7,000 Mormons crossed Nebraska in 1847. Their first party left the Elkhorn on April 16, 1847 and consisted of 143 men and boys, 3 women and 2 children. They had 72 wagons, 93 horses, 52 mules, 66 oxen, 19 cows, 17 dogs and a few coops of chickens.

Their route took the north side of the Platte River. This was to keep distance between the Mormons and the *Gentiles* who would most likely be in pursuit of them. They arrived at their destination, a new Zion, which they called Salt Lake on July 24, 1847. The same year over 6,000 *Gentiles* went through the Platte River valley on their way to California and Oregon.

It is thought that the Mormons were not well equipped for their journey, but they generally made better time and suffered less in the way of hardships. The following year, 1848, Brigham Young led approximately 2,500 emigrants to Salt Lake. Once again, their official trail was on the north side of the Platte. However, some did use the South Platte trail.

In 1855, Brigham Young announced that the church would no longer provide wagons for the emigrants. Instead handcarts were made and the emigrants were forced to walk the distance to their promised land. In this unusual trek the first group of about 500 persons left Florence in eastern Nebraska on July 17, 1856. One traveler described this as: "The carts were generally drawn by one man and three women each, though some carts were drawn by women alone. There were about three women to one man, and two-thirds of the women were single. It was the most motley crew I ever beheld. Most of them were Danes, with a sprinkling of Welsh, Swedes, and English, and were generally from the lower classes of their countries."

Between 1856 and 1860 there were ten handcart companies making the journey from Iowa City to Salt Lake City. The first with 274 persons, 52 handcarts and 5 wagons left Iowa City on June 9, 1856. There were 13 deaths reported enroute.

With a total of 2,962 emigrants and 653 handcarts, it would be impossible to detail each group passing through what would eventually become Lincoln County. However, a few of their recorded experiences are worth knowing about. Ellenor Roberts and Elias Lewis, ages 22 and 21 respectively, were married under a shade tree at an Iowa outfitting camp. As they began their journey to Zion they soon discovered that their handcart was much too full. They were forced to unload it and discard many of their precious items. Early in their journey they were faced with a scarcity of food. Ellenor's wedding ring was traded for flour.

When they reached the Missouri River, young Ellenor took off her shoes and set them on the bank. Once on the other side she recalled leaving them. She walked the rest of the way barefooted. They were among the members of the 3rd Company, better known as the Welsh Company, who journeyed in 1856.

The first handcart company rolled into Salt Lake City on September 26, 1855. The following year another 500 handcart emigrants left Florence. The last two companies were caught in the snows and out of the fifth company, 150 perished. The handcarts ceased to exist after 1860, with one expedition in 1859 and two in 1860 which was the final year.

The pioneers had a saying for the times they felt they could not go on. At that point they would say they had "seen the Elephant." Such is what happened to the party of the Burke-DeLong Wagon Train. In the spring of 1858, William Burke and his new wife, Janie DeLong, were in a wagon train which originated in Iowa. It consisted of at least four to six wagons of the Burke family and eight wagons of the DeLong family. The Burke wagons were drawn by horses with a remuda of spare horses along, while the DeLong wagons were drawn by oxen.

As the wagon train neared the confluence of the North and South Platte rivers east of what is now North Platte, the pioneers decided to cross to the north side. Approaching the area, one of the Burke wagons, possibly that of William Burke's grandparents, was in the lead, followed by his parent's wagon. Without much difficulty, the first two or three wagons forded the river. Since it was late afternoon, the lead wagons continued on to seek a place to camp for the night, leaving the others to continue crossing the river.

The wagons moved along the north bank of the North Platte River, out of sight of those fording it. William and Janie's wagon became mired in the sand. The DeLongs helped pull them out and some of the DeLong wagons continued on without difficulty. Suddenly one of the DeLong wagons became mired and dangerously tilted in the river. It had to be unloaded and pulled out, then reloaded. William Burke and his father-in-law, Willliam DeLong, stopped to assist.

Janie's mother walked back to William and Janie's wagon to visit. Once they started moving again, she remained in their wagon. They had barely started when they saw smoke rising in the distance and became suspicious. Driving horses, William and Janie reached the scene first. The lead wagons were burning and Indians were milling around. Some were riding away with the extra horses.

William thought if he charged them at full speed with his wagon they would run. Instead the remaining Indians attacked. An arrow hit Janie's mother in the neck and she was pulled from the wagon and scalped. William was bludgeoned in the shoulder and arm. Still holding the reins and his rifle, he was able to knock the Indian from the wagon.

The slower, ox-drawn DeLong wagons arrived shooting, which caused the Indians to flee. Everyone in the first wagons, except one bald-headed man, had been scalped. Some were not yet dead and lingered for days. Wagons had been set afire and some of the wounded in the wagons perished.

Janie DeLong Burke had seen the Elephant. The screams of the injured, trapped, and burning people in the wagons resounded in her ears. The smell of burning wagons and of death was putrid in her nostrils. The life that was in her womb quickened. Undaunted she and her husband kept going to California. Janie was never able to relieve her mind of that day when the setting sun screamed blood red. Each time she retold the story of the massacre along the North Platte River, she cried.

This constant, overflowing gush of civilization moving westward would not cease until 1869 with the completion of the transcontinental railroad system which linked the two coasts. Then the Oregon Trail became obsolete forever. However, the constant grinding of wagon wheels across the land created deep ruts in the Platte Valley, some still visible today ... constant reminders of the perseverance of our forefathers. Manifest destiny had been fulfilled.

CHAPTER 4

OLD SHORTER COUNTY

There was an effort made in 1844 to have the territory of Nebraska created. This move was defeated because those who favored slavery were alarmed by the prospect of the creation of a new free state.

On May 30, 1854, Congress passed the Kansas-Nebraska Act which was proposed by Senator Stephen A. Douglas. This provided for Kansas as a slave state and Nebraska as a free state. The first governor of the Territory of Nebraska, Francis Burt was selected by President Pierce, but died two weeks after he arrived. Thomas B. Cuming became acting governor of the territory. The first legislature met in Omaha City which had been founded in 1854 and served as the capital of the territory until statehood in 1867.

The territory actually included the present day state of Nebraska along with Kansas and portions of the Dakotas, Wyoming, Montana and Colorado. After the territory was created, more settlers began to pour into the area with the purpose of staying.

Until the late 1850s and early 1860s the Indians of the area caused only minor problems. Normally the war parties spotted by the emigrants were Sioux or Cheyennes on their way to attack Pawnees. The Indians became violent in the 1860s in retribution for the treaty violations in the Dakotas and Wyoming and the acts of violence by some of the immigrants. The hunting grounds of the Sioux and Cheyenne were beyond the forks of the Platte. The countless numbers of hungry emigrants passing through the Platte Valley had slaughtered many of the bison herds. This all combined to cause terror in the hearts of the native Americans.

In 1844 when travel along the Platte River was increasing, the first building was erected in what would eventually become Shorter County and later Lincoln County. It was built east of the confluence of the North and South Platte Rivers by a Frenchman. The building was constructed of cedar logs with iron doors and was used as a trading ranch or post. It was abandoned in 1848.

The first permanent settlement was made in 1858 at Cottonwood Springs. That fall a building was constructed by Isadore P. Boyer, Nelson Boyer and Joseph Robideaux to be used as a trading post. Isadore P. Boyer was in charge. He was still at this location when the 1860 Territorial Census was taken in June of 1860. Nelson Boyer, his brother, died of convulsions sometime during the census year. The Boyers were French and Joseph Robideaux was their uncle. They came from Illinois via St. Joseph, Missouri. The 1860 Territorial Census shows that Isadore was born in Missouri. They were the first white men to settle within the boundaries of what is now Lincoln County.

They used cedar logs from the canyons and built a good-sized trading post with a large stable. It was all enclosed with a solid log stockade. They used a long island in the Platte River for grazing their cattle and obtained water from a nearby spring. Robideaux left shortly after they settled there, returning to St. Joseph, Missouri.

The locale was named Cottonwood Springs because of the location of a spring surrounded by a large grove of cottonwood trees. This comprised a tract of land of approximately 100 acres and was located at Nebraska Pony Express Station No. 21 just east of the Cottonwood Creek. It was first called Cottonwood and in 1860 changed to Cottonwood Falls. Three months later the name was changed to Cottonwood Springs.

On January 7, 1860 at Cottonwood Springs, a county was created that included almost the western half of what we know today as the state of Nebraska. It also included what eventually became Colorado and Wyoming ... and was called Shorter County. The government was somewhat loosely constructed or perhaps the citizens of the newly formed county had other things than government on their minds. The first officers were Charles McDonald as judge; Washington Mallory Hinman as treasurer; Isadore P. Boyer, J.C. Gilman and John (Jack) A. Morrow as commissioners.

These officers having failed, with two or three exceptions, to qualify, and no elections having been held, the organization of the county was practically of no effect. The first known transaction of legal government took place September 3, 1866 when a meeting was held to reorganize Shorter County. Under Territorial laws of Nebraska it was reorganized and named Lincoln County in honor of President Abraham Lincoln. An election was held on October 9, 1866 with the following officers elected: S.D. Fitchie, Judge; William Baker, Sheriff; Charles McDonald, Clerk and Commissioners J.C. Gilman, Washington Mallory Hinman and John A. (Jack) Morrow. The county seat under both county names was Cottonwood Springs.

The western settlements of the United States not only needed supplies and freight, but also mail. Mail arrived in California via the ocean route. This left the mountainous settlement without any contact. Year after year with more settlements between the Mississippi and the Pacific Ocean, the demand was greater for better mail service. In 1859 mining communities in the Pike's Peak region of Colorado added impetus to this demand. William H. Russell conceived the idea of having stage coach express to the Pike's Peak region and with the aid of John S. Jones established the Leavenworth and Pike's Peak Express. After financial difficulty Russell, Majors and Waddell bailed the enterprise out and transferred the route to the Platte Valley, combining it with their Salt Lake mail service. More service came from the Western Stage Company which ran a weekly mail delivery over the Military Road from Omaha to Fort Kearny. Their services were extended to Denver in September of 1860.

The firm of Russell, Majors, Waddell & Co. engaged in freighting along the trail, operated 6,250 wagons with a team force of 75,000 oxen, and with a capital investment of $2,000,000. Their wagons were built by a St. Louis firm and had a storage and carrying capacity of 7,000 pounds. When they were fully loaded eight to ten yoke of oxen were required to pull them. A train of wagons consisted of 25 wagons.

In 1857, as an eleven year old in the employ of Russell, Majors and Waddell, William Frederick Cody (Buffalo Bill) accompanied a wagon train under the command of Lewis Simpson to Wyoming. There were no settlements in this area at that time. The Simpson train spent the winter at Fort Bridger after being captured by Lot Smith's Mormons on Big Sandy Creek. The following summer they returned to Leavenworth, Kansas. Cody went west again in the late spring of 1859 and doubtless saw a small settlement near the Platte River.

The 1860 Territorial Census for Shorter County shows three P.P. Express and California Stage Co. Stations, the P.P. standing for Pikes Peak. The locations of the eastern most one was probably around Brady or further east. The second one was possibly 3 miles west of Cottonwood and the third was probably located south of what would eventually become North Platte City.

William H. Russell was persuaded by Senator Gwin of California to start a Pony Express between St. Joseph, Missouri and California. Gwin promised to obtain a government mail contract for the Pony Express. The first Pony Express riders set out at both ends of the line on April 3, 1860. The mail came through in a scheduled 10 days.

The Pony Express primarily followed the route of the Oregon-California Trail. Along this were found stations about every fifteen miles. Riders covered 75 to 100 miles with a change of horses at each station. For the most part half-breed California mustangs were used and the riders were young men characteristically light weight, strong, courageous and with a knowledge of horsemanship and marksmanship. With the transcontinental telegraph, the Pony Express days were numbered. Since it was never a financial success it ceased to operate altogether on October 24, 1861. The government never made good on its promise of a mail contract. The Pony Express, however, did emphasize the importance of a central route and blazed a path for the transcontinental railroad linking the coasts. During the Civil War it also allowed California to remain in touch with the Union.

During the Civil War the Butterfield Overland Mail was transferred to the central Platte Valley route. Letter mail went through in 20 days and other mail in 35 days. Ben Holladay purchased the line in 1862 and improved and extended its service. In 1866 Wells, Fargo purchased the line and continued to run mail until the railroad was completed.

Swaying coaches drawn by four to six horses or mules traversed the Platte River Valley during the Civil War years. The Concord coaches were manufactured by Abbott-Downing of Concord, New Hampshire and carried as many as nine passengers. They carried mail and express and averaged about 6 miles per hour through the Platte River Valley. During the Civil War passage from the Missouri River, via the Platte River Valley to Denver cost $175, nearly 37 cents per mile.

In 1865 the stage route was described by Massachusetts editor, Samuel Bowles, as having a stable every 10 to 15 miles, along with an eating house. Every 50 to 100 miles there was a small grocery and blacksmith shop. By 1865 he recorded there were military stations along the way. Bowles stated, "This makes up all the civilization of the Plains." Bowles was witnessing the destiny of the valley of the Platte River. He wrote "...it is on the line of our great cities and our great industries, East and West."

Congress authorized the Secretary of the Treasury in June of 1860 to subsidize a telegraph line from west Missouri to San Francisco.

On November 18, 1860 Edward Creighton, acting as general agent for Western Union, left Omaha to make plans for the telegraph's extension westward. A California company was to build the western end of the telegraph line and the Pacific Telegraph Company, under liberal incorporation laws of the Nebraska territory, would construct the eastern end, meeting at Salt Lake City. During the spring of 1861 the line from Fort Kearny to Julesburg was completed.

The treeless prairie of western Nebraska posed a problem. Hundreds of wagons were used to transport wire, tools and provisions west from Missouri. Cedar poles cut from the canyons at Cottonwood Springs were used for many miles of the line.

It was no accident that the first dwellings were established as road ranches or stations. They were built along the south side of the Platte River to accommodate the travelers to California and other points west. Their business was profitable and lasted until the coming of the railroad. The only farming done by these early settlers was an acre or so for themselves. Their livelihood was derived from boarding and tending to the needs of the travelers. Many of the road ranches had a general store with commodities, such as clothes, food stuffs and provisions to get the traveler further west.

The road ranche proprietors traded in a variety of goods including oxen for trail-worn horses or mules which would be rested, nourished and traded once again. As evidenced by the 1860 Territorial Census for Shorter County herders were hired by the station or ranch owners to keep the cattle near headquarters and away from any marauding Indians. Cattle would also stray into buffalo herds. As evidenced by the real estate and property values of those station/road ranch owners on the 1860 Territorial Census, they prospered.

The road ranche stations also traded with the Indians, exchanging their goods and ornaments for buffalo, beaver and other furs. Indians would pay a premium price for firearms and ammunition, exchanging furs and ponies for them. It was common for the traders to offer presents to the Indians as an enticement for trading transactions. When a tribe came into the area to trade, the chiefs would visit all the trading stations. The Indians were fed and while they drank coffee the trader would pour flour, sugar and food articles into a sack suspended from their shoulders. According to the *HISTORY OF THE STATE OF NEBRASKA* by Andreas these feasts often cost the trader $50 to $100. If he was selected for the trading, the profits would be enormous.

O'Fallons Bluff was located about 325 miles from Omaha and 25 to 30 miles from the junction of the Platte Rivers. It was a hinderance to travelers along the Oregon Trail as well as the freighters in the area. Emigrants on their way to California and Oregon had to cross the South Platte River to reach the south bank of the North Platte River. They were encumbered much of the time by high water, marshes and the numerous channels in the South Platte River. O'Fallons Bluff, located south of the present town of Sutherland, stood as an obstacle.

The travelers had to cross the bluffs and descend to the valley below, adding a full day to their travel time.

The "Omaha Nebraskian" of 1859 revealed that there was a trading post, a stage station with plenty of wood, water, grass and hay at O'Fallons Bluff. Some historians state that the bluffs were named after a hunter, soldier and agent named Major Benjamin O'Fallon. He was a government agent to the Missouri tribes. Records indicate that he possessed remarkable knowledge of Indian customs, habits and characteristics and that he was brave to the point of foolhardiness. He was supposedly killed at the bluff site by Cheyenne Indians. In 1856 three men from Council Bluffs were killed there by Indians. Other historical accounts indicate that the bluffs were named for a hunter killed there. Major O'Fallon's death remains somewhat of a mystery.

The bluffs were definitely known for ambushes since they came almost to the river. Because of the Indian skirmishes, a detachment of troops was stationed in the area. By 1866 the troops sent to O'Fallons Bluff had established Fort Heath. Little is known about the fort other than it was named for General H.H. Heath of the 7th Iowa Cavalry or his son, Lt. George W. Heath, who was killed at Cottonwood Springs in 1864.

An 1866 journal kept by Gurdon P. Lester mentions Fort Heath. A yellowed marriage license dated March 7, 1866 reveals that Theodore I. Parker and Lucinda A. Rogers, both of Cottonwood Springs, were married at Fort Heath. It is likely that Parker had been dispatched to Fort Heath from the fort at Cottonwood Springs.

It is believed that the actual O'Fallons Bluffs Station was located two miles south and four miles west of what is now Sutherland. This would have been in the southeast quarter of Section 3, Township 12 North, Range 34 West.

Sometime between July of 1864 and February 1865 the stage station was burned. The damage amounted to $3,500. The Indians also destroyed 65 sacks of corn which amounted to 7,280 pounds at 20 cents per pound, valued at $1,456, along with ten ton of hay valued at $400.

An interesting story about the Indians at O'Fallons Bluff has been preserved through the efforts of Eugene Ware. The Indians of the Platte Valley area were convinced that the telegraph wires were diabolical. One Indian felt he was most knowledgable about them and told the tribe that they were a good thing to have around. He planned to use the wire to lariat ponies.

He chopped down a pole, severed the wire and began ripping off the posts. The Indians then planned on taking the wire north with them to their village along the Blue Water River. They cut off almost a half-mile of wire and all of the Indians, riding in single file, held the wire, pulling it across the prairie to their village. It was during the hot summer and having gone several miles they were overtaken suddenly by an electrical storm. The story goes that a bolt of lightning knocked almost all of them off their horses and hurt many of them. The wire was subsequently dropped and they concluded that it was "bad medicine" and should be left alone.

In 1865 Charles E. Young who was passing through the area wrote, "The trail over the bluffs was of sand, and those heavily laden, white-covered prairie schooners would often sink to the hubs, requiring from fifty to seventy-five yoke of oxen to haul them across, often being compelled to double the leading yoke as far back as the wheelers, then doubling again, would start them on a trot, and with all in line and pulling together, would land the deeply sunken wheels on solid ground."

Another account of O'Fallons Bluff was written in the diary of E.H.N. Patterson and published in *Overland Routes to the Goldfield, 1859*. It relates, "Friday, May 20 (1859) Left camp at six o'clock; one mile brought us to a point where O'Fallons Bluffs strike the South Platte - where there is considerable brushwood and timber (the latter being on Shanghai Island), and the scenery is rough, rugged but romantic. The road now runs over the bluffs for three miles, to the stage station, where there is a trading post and some Indian tents. Wednesday, May 11, (camped east of Plum Creek) A man was carried down in a wagon today - one John Snyder, of Massilon, Ohio - mortally wounded, he having been shot near O'Fallons Bluff. The circumstances under which he received his wound are differently related; one report is that he was shot for robbing, whilst another is that he was shot and robbed."

The Boyers were not alone for long in the area of Cottonwood Springs. In 1859 William Bishop built a ranch with the aid of two Frenchmen, Vilantry and Gardipi. The Boyers resented their coming and tried to get them to locate farther west. After Bishop's store was built, the men formed a friendship which lasted until death. Bishop later located west of the area, and after the railroad went through, returned to Nebraska City.

In 1859 Dick Darling built the third building at Cottonwood Springs which was purchased by Charles McDonald for a store. McDonald completed the building in the fall of 1859, and brought his wife, Orra, from Omaha to his ranch in January of 1860. She was the first white woman to settle in the county. During 1860 several white women began coming to the county, but it was about three years before another white woman lived at Cottonwood Springs. According to the *HISTORY OF THE STATE OF NEBRASKA* by A.T. Andreas, the second white woman was a Mrs. Davis who lived a few miles from Cottonwood.

McDonald's ranch consisted of a cedar log store building, constructed about 200 yards south of the Boyer trading post. The main building was about 20 feet in front and 40 foot deep, two stories high. On the west was a 50 foot, one story, sod-roofed wing. A large corral was in the rear. There was a telegraph office in the stage station. The main building housed his store and saloon, with living quarters in the back. A large stockade enclosed the trading post, warehouse, stable and blacksmith shop. A square well, 40 feet deep, was in front of his store and between his and the Boyer's place. During the winter of 1859-1860 McDonald put in a large stock of supplies for freighters and emigrants.

Charles McDonald was born October 25, 1826 in Tennessee and came to Nebraska in 1855. In July of that year he located on a claim on Turkey Creek in Pawnee County. He later moved to Richardson County. On October 14, 1858, in Omaha, he married Orra B. Henry.

According to Orra McDonald's obituary, the McDonalds lived at Salem in Richardson County and then Fort Kearny after their marriage. The obituary reads that they came to Cottonwood Springs on August 23, 1860. However, they were enumerated there on June 13, 1860.

The first child, Frank, was born February 11, 1860, and died August 21, 1860. He is shown as the four-month old James on the census. The McDonalds are credited with having the first white child born in Shorter County when their son William H. McDonald was born June 14, 1861, at Cottonwood Springs. Some historians state that the first white child born there was Felix, son of Mr. and Mrs. Nelson Boyer. He was born in December of 1858, before the actual formation of the county. Some historians feel that the Boyers were not given credit for their son being the first white child born in the county because they were French.

Orra McDonald provided A.T. Andreas with a good deal of information when he wrote the history in 1882. She recalled that it was not uncommon to stand in the door of the ranch and count from 700 to 1,000 wagons pass in a single day. She also claimed to have counted 1,900 wagons passing the settlement at Cottonwood in one day. The Indians called her *Milla Huska*, meaning white squaw.

THE GREAT PLATTE RIVER VALLEY by Merrill J. Mattes contains information on the various sites of stations along the Platte River Valley.

About eight miles west of Gothenburg and on the far eastern border of Shorter (Lincoln) County was Gilman's, a Pony Express Station. It was also known as "Gillman's Ranche, Stage Station and Military Post." Apparently at some period of time there were soldiers occupying some of the log houses in that station area.

A site south of the present Brady is not mentioned in the mail contract for the Pony Express. It was, however, called by a variety of names such as Dan Trout's Station, Joe Bower's Ranche and Boken Ranche. The main two story log building was called Machette's. In 1854 it was used as a trading post. In 1931 the building was dismantled and taken to Gothenburg where it was rebuilt and was called a Pony Express Station.

The 1860 Territorial Census for Shorter County shows a trader named Samuel Machett living east of Cottonwood Springs. It was identified as "J. Machette's trading post" in the "*Guide to the Gold Mines*" carried in the Council Bluffs' *Daily Telegraph* of April 9, 1861. This article also places it at or near Cottonwood Springs in competition with McDonald. There were approximately six miles between the two given sites and 16 miles between Gilman's and Cottonwood. Because of the distance between those two points, it seems questionable that there would be a Pony Express site at Machette's. Undoubtedly though, there was some type of road ranche in that area.

Approximately three miles from the Machette station area south of Brady was located the Fox Station or Frost's Ranche. The buildings were constructed of cedar and adobe. Three miles further west was located the Cottonwood Springs area and an overland stage station discussed previously. It was sometimes referred to as McDonald's Station or McDonald and Clark's Ranche. This was located midway between Fort Kearny and Juleburg and was later the site of a military fort.

A couple of miles further was the Fitchie's Ranch. Very close by was the Box Elder Stage Station and Telegraph Office. One-half mile south was the Ronan Ranche and in the same close vicinity was Justus S. North's Ranche. In that approximate area the 1860 Territorial Census shows a John S. North, station keeper for the P.P. Express and California Stage Co. Station.

One mile down the trail was the Hindman or Hinman Ranche. This may have been the Charles Hinman of the 1860 Territorial Census or another of the early Hinmans in the area. Just below the confluence of the North Platte and South Platte Rivers was a famous ranche called Jack Morrow's Ranche or Station. It was also known as the Junction House.

Directly south of the present city of North Platte was a Pony Express and stage station called Cold Springs or Cold Springs Ranche and Stage Station. It was constructed of cedar and adobe. Halfway between that and the present community of Hershey was the Fremont Station which was opposite Fremont's Slough. It was also known as the Bishop's Station or Bishop's Ranch and later was known as Beer's Ranch.

At the site of the Lower Crossing of the South Platte and opposite the present community of Hershey was the Fremont Springs Pony Express and Stage Station. It was also known as Buffalo Ranch. The structure of the building did not match others in the area as it was built in a style peculiar to the south. Two huts were connected by a roofwork of thatched timber which acted as a verandah.

O'Fallons Bluff Station or the Military Post had been established early and was east of the actual bluff bearing the same name, south of the present Sutherland. Also opposite Sutherland and just below O'Fallons Bluff was Bob William's Ranche. Directly at the bluffs was the Moore's Ranche or O'Fallon Road Ranche. By 1866 the adobe walls were in ruin. Within a few years it was called the Lou Baker road ranche and known for frequent Indian attacks. It is undoubtedly the location of Crawford Moore, the first person enumerated on the 1860 Territorial Census for Shorter County.

CHAPTER 5

PLATTE VALLEY CHARACTERS

A road ranche located just each of Brady Island was known as the Gilman Ranch. It was owned and operated by brothers, John and Jeremiah Gilman, who were fifth great grandchildren of the immigrant, Edward Gilman, who had arrived in Boston in 1638. The ranch became not only a trading post, but also a Pony Express Station, a stage station and at times an army post.

The brothers, who were originally from New Hampshire, had owned a livery stable in Nebraska City until 1859, when they sold out and headed west for the gold fields. It was an accident that they located where they did. Near the mouth of a gulch located approximately 15 miles east of Cottonwood Springs, their wagon broke down. While it was being repaired they noticed the constant traffic in the area, going in both directions, and decided to stay. They put up sod and log buildings and dug a good well which they topped with an iron pump. This became a landmark along the trail. The Indians named John Gilman, *We-chox-cha* which meant *old man with the pump*.

Before long the Gilmans were speaking the Sioux and Cheyenne languages, enough so that they could carry on a good trade in hides and furs with the Indians. During 1860 and 1861 their ranch became a station for the Pony Express. While the fort was being constructed the brothers assisted by furnishing supplies. The brothers also furnished poles for the Creighton telegraph being built across Nebraska. As progress accelerated, they supplied ties for the construction of the Union Pacific railroad.

Jeremiah Gilman was the first sheriff of Shorter County, being elected in 1860. He was elected as one of the commissioners in 1866 when it was reorganized to Lincoln County. The Gilman brothers left Lincoln County in 1868 as rich men and made their homes in Nebraska City.

According to some records, there was a stage station and ranch located in the vicinity of Snell Canyon, east of Cottonwood Springs. The exact date is unknown, but a Jacob Snell kept a stage station there which he purchased from "Billy" Hill. He kept horses for the frequent relay of the stage line and also fed the drivers and passengers. This land later was owned by E.E. Ericsson.

Washington Mallory Hinman, who was born in 1819 in Pennsylvania, first saw the Platte Valley in 1849 on his way to

California. He returned from California in 1854. Many records indicate that he had settled at Cottonwood Springs by 1860 where he set up a general supply store, steam sawmill, shingle mill and blacksmith shop.

The 1860 Territorial Census shows a Charles Hinman, age 25 in that particuar area of Shorter County. He also was born in Pennsylvania. There were three squaw men in the county and Charles Hinman was one of them. Living with him was an Indian woman named Clara. According to Hinman family records, Washington M. Hinman was in the county very early and lived with a couple of Indian wives. They recall their names as *Laughing Eyes* and *Big Mouth*. Washington Hinman would have been age 40 in 1860. The family has nothing on record which indicates a relationship to this Charles Hinman.

On September 14, 1863 at Cottonwood Springs, Washington Hinman married Virginia Hill, also of Cottonwood Springs. They are both shown on the marriage license as being age 21, whereas his actual age should have been 44. His birthday was that same day. The couple were married by Judge Charles McDonald and the ceremony was witnessed by H.C. Wright. Family members indicate that Virginia Hill did not live long and no children were apparently born by that marriage.

Washington Hinman was county treasurer for Shorter County when it was created in 1860. Descendants state that he told of carrying the county records around in his hat and later stored them in his home. Hinman spoke the Sioux language fluently and after the establishment of Fort McPherson became an interpreter. He had a contract to furnish lumber for the buildings at the fort as well as beef. A single voucher in the amount of $14,000 for these services has survived. When the county was reorganized into Lincoln County he became one of the first commissioners.

In 1867 he returned to Pennsylvania to marry Rebecca Franklin Vaughan. Soon after the establishment of North Platte, Wash Hinman built a log house there for his family. Most of the commissioner's meetings were held in that house. According to some records, their son Vaughn, was the first white child born in North Platte. In 1879 Wash moved to his farm west of town where he died January 27, 1904.

From about 1860 to 1862 Washington's brother, Beach Isaac Hinman was associated with him in business. In 1862 Beach went to Plattsmouth, Nebraska to resume his law practice. In 1864 he went to Montana where he was engaged in mining until 1868. He returned to the area in 1869, settling at North Platte. Another brother, John F. Hinman came to North Platte in 1865, working for two years on the railroad. He managed a construction firm and did contracting. He left for Texas, returning to North Platte in 1877.

Living very close to the Cottonwood area in 1860 was a William S. Comstock. He was a guide, interpreter and well-known buffalo hunter. In 1868 he was located at Fort Wallace. William Frederick Cody had earned a reputation by then as being one of the best buffalo hunters, so much so that he gained the nickname *Buffalo Bill*. Cody was stationed at Fort Hays during the same period of time. A contest for the title of *Champion Buffalo Hunter of the Plains* ensued.

This resulted in a famous shooting match, with cash bets and support from the various officers of the two posts. The hunt was advertised as far away as St. Louis, Missouri. The billings read that it would take place for the the *Championship of the World* and $500. About 100 gentlemen and ladies of St. Louis came west on a special train to witness it.

The final tally showed Cody had killed 69 buffalo and Comstock had killed 46. There has been some confusion amongst historians whether the contest ever took place as there is little documentation regarding it. Cody and his wife were apparently the only eyewitnesses to report on it. At any rate, the same William Comstock had lived briefly in Shorter County when it was first formed.

Of all the road ranches or stations along the trail, that of John "Jack" Morrow was the most notorious. In the late 1850s he was a government teamster, freighting from Omaha to Denver and on to Salt Lake City. Morrow was always known as a bully, scoundrel and thief. It was thought that he stole from his loads to later resell the goods for his own profit.

When he first came to the Platte River area he entered into partnership with old Constant, a Frenchman, at Dog Town which was near Fort Kearny. Morrow left there with old Constant swearing he had been robbed.

His ranch was established by 1860 and located on the prairie, about one-half mile south of the confluence of the Platte rivers. It was located against the rugged bluffs on the south edge of the valley. His ranchhouse was built from logs hauled from nearby Moran Canyon. The dwelling was 60 feet long and 2 1/2 stories high. The top story was divided into several rooms. However, the cross logs were not sawed out to make doors, thus his roomers or boarders had to crawl over the tops of six foot high walls to get between the rooms. Even so, many people paid to stay at his ranch on their way west or east.

Morrow supposedly cut out 5,000 cedar logs from Moran Canyon for his own use and to sell to other persons. He also cut out 2,000 fine cedar telegraph poles. He forbid people from cutting timber in the canyon for their own use. His claim was to have had cattle and goods along with improvements worth $100,000, which was probably overestimated.

In the book, THE INDIAN WAR OF 1864 by Ware, he is described as being tall, raw-boned and dangerous looking. He had a mustache and a goatee. John Bratt in his TRAILS OF YESTERDAY stated that Morrow wore a diamond in his "yellow and badly soiled shirt bosom." This diamond was said to have been valued at $1,000. Morrow was also noted as a killer, supposedly having shot a man or two. Traditionally Morrow had a fight with the Irish desperado, Murphy, and killed him. Morrow is described in other historical accounts as being a slight person, with light hair and brown eyes and of medium height. Fighting men generally regarded him as a bluffer.

The ranch was often called the Junction Ranch because of its location at the confluence of the rivers. Emigrants were forewarned about the ranch. The Indians stampeded the area which added to its bad reputation. If the Indians didn't steal the teams and livestock, the emigrants took a chance by staying there that Morrow would rob them of their money and valuables. Because of this, many of the wagon trains would follow the river bank one-half mile to the north.

Morrow dug a deep ditch and dike all the way from his ranch to the river except for a narrow crossing in front of his ranchhouse. Between Fort Cottonwood and Morrow's ranch ran a range of high hills that were broken by a sort of peak which was called Point Lookout or Sioux Lookout. It was known that Morrow would be signaled from Sioux Lookout a few miles east of the ranch to inform him of approaching wagon trains. If they camped nearby, it was easy to move their cattle and horses into the hills behind the ranch. Once they were hidden, Morrow would call upon the emigrants, offer his condolances and the sale of his "high priced" replacement stock. Most of that stock had been stolen from previous wagon trains.

The Indians traded with him and he acquired a good stock of furs, hides, and dried meats. These he would take in an annual, long wagon caravan to Omaha. Once the merchandise was sold Morrow went on a drunken spree which was talked about all the way back to Denver.

Eventually Morrow put his ranch foreman, Hugh "Hewey" Morgan, in charge of the ranch, while he traveled up and down overseeing his affairs. Morgan had a good reputation and was eventually elected treasurer of Lincoln County in 1866 and 1867. Morgan is listed next door to John A. "Jack" Morrow on the 1860 Territorial Census of Shorter County.

Morrow was elected county commissioner of old Shorter County in 1860, but little business was transacted for him to have made an impact upon the county. Some remember him as a squaw man and there were stories that his Indian wives were buried under the hill at the back of his ranch. By 1866 he reportedly had a white wife. If they were married in Shorter (Lincoln) County, a license or record never survived. Bratt describes Morrow's wife as being a modest, refined, neatly-dressed woman, out of place in her surroundings.

The extravagant Morrow enjoyed the best of food and wine and kept champagne at his ranch. He served it to guests in tin cups along with broiled antelope heart, baked buffalo hump and fried beaver tails. One time he bragged at Fort McPherson, while drunk, that he came from Missouri and got into whacking bulls across the plains. He then got onto a government train loaded with ammunition and unscrewed the boxes. Apparently he then took out the ammunition and sold it to ranchmen, filling the boxes with sand and screwing them down. He caused a rumpus with the wagon master before they got to Laramie and took off before they suspected what he had done.

In 1869 the valley was well settled and at that time he was "warned out" by the commander of Fort McPherson. Morrow returned to Omaha where he had a fancy home and became a railroad and government contractor, a general speculator. His wealth had supposedly been gained in Omaha taking contracts and playing poker with visiting Congressmen. He reportedly won $60,000 in one night. Morrow died in Omaha, having greatly wasted his once large fortune.

Another interesting character of the Platte Valley was Sam Fitchie. He did some residing at the Junction Ranch in the 1860s. He is not shown on the 1860 Territorial Census so apparently came shortly thereafter. He could recite poetry and was an impersonator, rather well-educated. Early marriage records reveal that Fitchie was a probate judge in 1866.

The traders remained at their ranches, but also sent men and supplies out to the Indian villages to trade for moccasins, robes and other commodities. John Corlew and Will Kirby who kept a ranch near O'Fallons Bluff, were known to have done this. They were, unlike Morrow, considered to be honorable of intent.

The 1860 Territorial Census Mortality Schedule reflects the death of one A.S. Dow who was an emigrant struck by lightning. He was Augustus S. Dow who moved from Sycamore, Illinois to Boone County, Iowa in 1854. In June of 1860, while on a wagon train for a business trip to Denver, he was killed by lightning. It was estimated that this occurred about 125 miles west of Fort Kearny. His companions dug his grave and buried him in his blanket, marking the spot with cedar posts on which they cut his name, place of residence and cause of his death.

About six years after his burial, the site was selected for the burying ground adjacent to Fort McPherson. In 1885 the cedar posts were still standing, but little could be read of the inscription. A rough stone bearing the name "Dow" was placed on the grave at that time. His name was entered in the record book of the Fort McPherson National Cemetery.

The 1860s, not unlike the two decades early, provided no extra comfort or facilities for the burying of the dead. They were most often buried in a grave which, unless recorded in a journal or diary, would be lost in the passing of time both to recognition and memory.

A member of a wagon party passing west through the Platte River Valley recorded a death which would later be remembered and recognized. Amongst the wagon party was the Rev. Benjamin F. Wade and family of Wapello County, Iowa. They were on their way to Oregon. On June 1865 the wagon train party camped for the night about eight miles west of Cottonwood Springs.

Providing encamp entertainment, there were several men in the group who were good violinists. The young people in the group began to dance to the music. Their tunes included *"The Arkansas Traveler"* and *"The Girl I Left Behind Me."*

The Rev. Wade remarked early in the evening, "Before morning some of them may be weeping." His words turned out to be a prophecy. Rev. Wade was to stand guard for the party that night. With gun in hand and a blanket over his shoulder, he reported and was allotted his beat. Later he was chilled by the night air and without saying anything to the guard next to him, went to his wagon to get a heavier blanket.

Later on he went out beyond his beat and sat down. When he arose to come back to his post, the other guard, Tom Lower, saw the figure arise and move. He mistook him for a prowling Indian. Lower asked, "Who's there?" Wade replied "A friend, don't shoot." It was windy that evening and Lower didn't hear the answer. He shot, wounding Wade.

A party was sent to get the army surgeon from the fort. The surgeon dressed the wounds and Rev. Wade was taken to the army hospital at the fort. He died June 3, 1865. Wade's family continued with the wagon train, settling in Silverton, Oregon.

Descendants placed a marker on his grave which was located in what is now the Plainview Cemetery south of Maxwell. The marker reads that he was a United Brethren Circuit Rider and that he was born about 1815 and died June 3, 1865.

Irish born John McCullough came to the Brady area in 1865 as a hunter for the railroad track layers. He was the first water pumper for the Union Pacific railroad. By 1866 he had opened a general store in a soddie. It was in 1867 at the Brady depot that he met Mary Ann Gallagher. She was engaged at the time to Major Frank North. McCullough wooed her from North and married her in January of 1869 at McPherson (Maxwell).

During the time that Fort McPherson was in operation John "Mac" McCullough had a hotel three and one-half miles north of the fort. When soldiers came for mail and supplies they would water their horses and get a cold drink of water from his well. Soon the word got around that they could drink from Mac's well. According to some historical reporting, the Mac's well was varied to the spelling, Maxwell, which became the name for the town which developed there. According to *NEBRASKA PLACE NAMES* by Lilian L. Fitzpatrick, the site was originally called McPherson after the nearby fort. Her records indicate it was named Maxwell for an early official on the Union Pacific.

Ben Gallagher was the first settler or post trader at Fort McPherson in late 1863. He eventually, in 1868, bought out the Gilmans when they returned to eastern Nebraska. Gallagher established a chain of trading posts to the east and by 1869 was well known in the cattle business.

Another early settler in the county was John Burke. He came with his wife and baby son, Daniel, from Germany to New Orleans in 1852. They settled in Minnesota, then Illinois. Eight years later they came to Tecumseh, Nebraska Territory. While living in Tecumseh the Burkes were attacked by the Kansas Jayhawkers and robbed of $1,000, 26 head of cattle and 22 horses along with many provisions.

Having freighted through Nebraska to Julesburg for a few years, around 1864 Burke and his family started for the gold fields of Colorado. With rumors of many Indian attacks in the Colorado area, he decided to stay, did some farming, sold grain and vegetables to the Oregon Trail travelers and built the first irrigation ditch in the western portion of Nebraska. Their water came from the south side of the Platte River located near their ranch. He also had contracts for wood and hay with the Union Pacific Railroad and the United States Government. In addition, the Burkes handled mail contracts for the railroad and Fort McPherson.

Their first ranch was attacked by Indians who ran off all the livestock and destroyed and burned the buildings. The Burke family escaped to the fort. John Burke then bought the Fitchie road ranch and the old Ben Holladay Stage Station which was located about two miles west of the fort. Their home of red cedar logs was the house Holladay had used to accommodate this stage line employees and where passengers were fed. About 100 yards to the south on a little rise was the location of a saloon used in the stage station days. The portion of Burke's log house facing that saloon was a solid wall with no windows or openings.

A major obstacle in the freighting business of that area was the Platte River. At that time the Platte had four main channels. There were a few toeheads sparsely covered with thickets of willow and plum. These were on the three shallow south channels which were often dry in the fall of the year. The north channel of the river was very swift and deep throughout the year. Some records indicate it was 400 feet wide and 15 feet deep with a fast and treacherous current. The quicksand there and in the other three channels made the Platte dangerous to ford.

To facilitate the freighting business between Fort McPherson and McPherson Station, John Burke decided in 1866 to bridge the north channel of the Platte River. He bought a quantity of surplus government freight wagon running gears, dragged them into the river and lined them up parallel, with tongues pointing downstream. Cedar logs were then placed crosswise on the wagons, then another layer lengthwise, and another crosswise, until he had a "crib" high enough to clear the water. Over the top layer Burke laid split logs, brush and hay, thus making a roadway on which teams and wagons could traverse. This became the first wagon bridge built across the Platte River within the present state boundaries of Nebraska. This makeshift, narrow structure was uneven, with many gaps and holes in its floor. A toll was charged for crossing it and because of this and its structure, many people chanced their luck at fording the river. Soldiers usually swam their horses across.

Even so, the Burkes hauled tons of firewood for the Union Pacific and freight for Fort McPherson across their bridge. Doing so they usually received $4 a cord for the wood which they laid down in the railroad woodyard and 45 cents per 100 for the freight.

The first bridge was doomed with the annual spring flood. The Platte, on its rampage, running wide to the hills on either side, soon destroyed the bridge. In the winter of 1869 Burke replaced it with one built on driven cedar piles. This pile bridge, while somewhat better than its predecessor and higher above the water, still lacked conveniences. There were no side rails and the floor logs were not spiked to the stringers.

John Burke saw to it that the freight went through regardless of the condition of his bridges or the flood level of the Platte River. During the flood season of 1872, he put a flat boat into the river. In June of that year, while crossing with a load of heavy freight some crates shifted, capsizing the boat. John Burke and one of his men drowned. He and his wife, Margaret, who died years later, are buried side by side in the Plainview Cemetery. This cemetery was located on a corner of the Burke land, within plain sight of the old log house.

J. Sterling Morton commented about Burke, "He was honest, generous to a fault, knew no fear, and no one was ever turned away from his ranch without a meal. Rich or poor they were always welcome, especially the officers and soldiers of the Fort, who held Mr. Burke and family in highest regard, and for whom nothing was too good."

After their father's death, his sons repaired the bridge and continued to operate the freight line until Fort McPherson was discontinued. It is interesting to note that later when county engineers began to build bridges they could find no better crossing of the Platte than where John Burke had built his bridge. Their bridge was built about 40 feet to the west of the old cedar bridge.

Sandbars and toeheads covered with tall trees, thickets and brush choke the north channel of the Platte River today. The ever shifting sands along with the heavy growth of brush and trees eventually covered the old wagon wheels used for Burke's bridge. They became buried in the middle of the once swift river. When the sand shifts in the right direction and the water level is low, portions of them can still be seen.

In 1866 John Bratt was working as a bullwhacker on the Overland Trail. He wrote that by the time they reached Fort McPherson that year they had passed several bandoned or burned ranches. He mentioned those of Peniston and Miller and the Gilman brothers. Bratt recalled that seeking shelter at the fort were John Burke and family, E.E. Ericsson, Sam Fitchie and others. While John Bratt recalls seeing Ericsson at the fort in 1866, the biographical sktch pertaining to him in *AN ILLUSTRATED HISTORY OF LINCOLN COUNTY, NEBRASKA AND HER PEOPLE* states that Ericsson was in Nebraska City in 1866, coming to Lincoln County in 1867. He became the first homesteader in Lincoln County, with his farm serving as a stage station.

Bratt's wagon train was halted at the fort and their arms and ammunition examined. Their force was strengthened by two additional ox trains loaded with government supplies for Fort Laramie. Bratt stated that they followed the south bank of the Platte River ... a mile wide and "bank full of yellowish muddy water." Their meals of beans, coffee, bacon, syrup and Dutch oven bread were enhanced with fish they caught and deer, antelope and buffalo they shot.

As Bratt and his group traveled west of the fort they passed what was left of the Burke ranch. The Indians had taken everything of value and then burned their buildings. Bratt comments, "Little did I dream at that time that the little blue-eyed daughter, who came so near being captured, would one day become my wife."

In his book, TRAILS OF YESTERDAY, Bratt comments that there were several hundred Sioux Indians at Jack Morrow's ranch along with squawmen and other people. He names Jack Sharp, Bob Rowland, Tod Randall, Turgeon and other noted Sioux-speaking frontiersmen. Bratt makes mention of Morrow's dike which he dug to prevent any freighting or emigrant wagons from traveling north of his road ranche. While passing through that area Bratt was approached by a squaw who offered him a little Indian boy for a plug of tobacco. The boy was naked save for a string of beads around his neck. The exchange was not made.

John Bratt was born in England and came to America in 1864 at the age of 21. He spent five adventurous years along the Oregon Trail from Omaha to Fort Laramie in the employ of Isaac Coe and Levi Carter. He later went into partnership with them in the cattle business, eventually locating at a ranch north of the Jack Morrow road ranche. On May 18, 1875, at Cottonwood Springs he married Elizabeth "Lizzie" Burke, daughter of John and Margaret Burke ... the little blue-eyed girl he had seen years earlier at the fort. They were married by the post chaplin, C.L. Hequembourg. The Bratts lived on the ranch four and one-half miles southeast of North Platte, raising a family of four daughters. John Bratt died in 1918 and Elizabeth Burke Bratt died in 1937.

CHAPTER 6

MESSERS. PALLERDY AND MORIN

Two Frenchmen whose lives would eventually become entwined in the settlement and history of the Platte Valley were Leon Pallerdy and Edward de Morin.

One of the best Sioux interpreters on the plains, Pallerdy was baptized Francois Leon Pallardie at St. Charles, Missouri in January of 1831. He was the son of Pierre and Eulalie Sarie Pallardie. The father, Pierre, was born at St. Charles in 1800 and was a noted hunter. Pierre had three wives and 21 children, Leon being the third child and eldest of 12 by his second wife. Leon's surname is often shown as Palliday.

As a teen, Leon Pallerdy started in the fur trade business with noted St. Charles fur traders, James Bordeaux, Nicholas and Antoine Janis and G.P. Beauvais. Nicholas "Nick" Janis would eventually become the trail agent for part of the Sioux at the battle of Massacre Canyon in Nebraska.

Pallerdy may have been in this area as early as 1845 when he was age 14. In 1849 he was traveling in a one-horse, rudely constructed wagon when on May 25th near Courthouse Rock he met up with a wagon train. He then joined traders living near Scotts Bluff. That fall he worked as a trapper at Bent's Fort in the southeast Colorado area.

In partnership with Augustine Lucian (Lucia) he ran a small trading post in 1854 in the area which is now Sidney, Nebraska. Lucian was an interpreter for Lt. Grattan on August 19, 1854 when he and his troops were massacred by the Sioux east of Fort Laramie. Pallerdy became guardian of the half-breed Lucian children. Some he provided with a formal education in the east. One of Lucian's daughters married Mortimer Harrison "Monty" Clifford and lived in Frontier County, Nebraska. Lucian's Indian widow is buried in the cemetery at Stockville in Frontier County.

Pallerdy worked as a clerk and trader for G.P. Beauvais in the 1860s. He scouted and translated for the military at Fort Laramie and Camp Cottonwood. Except for the years 1870-1872 he was the main scout at Camp Cottonwood (Fort McPherson). He was replaced at the fort during those two years by William F. "Buffalo Bill" Cody. In the late 1860s he served as a Brule Sioux interpreter at the Fort Laramie peace councils and made several trips to Washington, D.C. To the Sioux, Pallerdy was known as *The Wolf*.

In December of 1872 when Cody went into show business, Leon became the main scout at Fort McPherson. All the while he continued his trading and business with the Indians. During the first three months of 1873 he made two trips to the Republican River country. He took one outfit of goods to the Chief Creek area of Dundy County and a second to Sinking Water. In August of that year Capt. Charles Meinhold made an expedition to the Republican Valley and discovered the aftermath of the Battle of Massacre Canyon. Pallerdy guided the troops and took a small force in pursuit of the Sioux. He also served as a guide to the Loup River country.

On November 6, 1867 Pallerdy married young Valentine Morin, daughter of Edward and Valentine Peater/Peters de Morin. They were married in a gala wedding in the Union Pacific Hotel in North Platte City. Their marriage certificate shows that Leon was age 36, residing at North Platte, and Valentine was age 16, of Cottonwood Springs. They were married by Washington Mallory Hinman and the wedding was witnessed by General W.T. Sherman, General J.B. Sanborn and others. These two generals were in Lincoln County, along with other officers, to negotiate a peace treaty with the Indians. Historical accounts relate that General Sherman was awarded the honor of being the first to kiss the bride.

In 1875 Pallerdy began construction of a house for his wife in North Platte. This was located in the area where the Pawnee Hotel is now located in North Platte. During the same period of time he acted as an interpretor, taking Indians to Washington, D.C. and also got caught up in the gold fever in the Black Hills. Pallerdy's marriage ended in divorce. There are no surviving records in the courthouse in North Platte of this divorce, but it occurred between 1875 and 1878.

He went to the Black Hills, but ended up working among the Ogallala Sioux at the Red Cloud Agency. Eventually he married an Indian woman named Alice. Little is known about the later years of Pallerdy's life other than that he worked at various jobs in the Indian Agency in Pine Ridge, South Dakota. He was killed in a fight at Chadron sometime prior to 1893. His place of burial is unknown.

As for Valentine Morin Pallerdy, she remarried on March 4, 1878 at North Platte to Joseph F. Fillion. Her marriage certificate shows her name as Mrs. Valenteen Morin, age 26. The Fillions resided in North Platte. Valentine apparently had no children, or at least any who survived, by Pallerdy. She did, however, have children by Fillion.

Edward de Morin was born in 1818 in Montreal, Canada to French-Canadian parents. His father was a voyageur and trader on the St. Lawrence River. Their name has often been spelled simply as Morin or Moran.

At the age of 16, Edward was employed as a boatman at Fort Dearborn, Illinois (later Chicago). During the winter months, he trapped along the Illinois River. In the spring of 1836, Morin and some of his friends constructed a flotilla of boats, loaded them with furs and drifted down the Illinois and Mississippi Rivers to New Orleans.

When he returned to St. Louis he joined the American Fur Company and engaged in trading with the Indians along the Missouri River. During the winter of 1836-1837, Morin was left at a trading post near the mouth of the Niobrara River where he lived with the Ponca Indians for a few years.

In 1844, along with other hunters and trappers, he set out for California, but returned two years later to the Missouri River. In 1848 he was married in St. Louis to Valentine Peters, the daughter of a steamboat pilot on the Mississippi River.

Morin tired of the lazy drag of the keelboat along the rivers. For him the West was yet to be discovered and conquered. By 1853, they had settled in what would become Lincoln County in Nebraska Territory. The Morins are not shown on the 1860 Territorial Census for Shorter County. They may have been missed by the census taker or were briefly away from their home as several unoccupied dwellings were recorded. A decade earlier, Morin had enjoyed the solitude of this wilderness, traversing the plains and learning the ways of the Indians who called him *Iron Legs*.

Morin and his family established a trading post at the mouth of the Box Elder Canyon, approximately two miles west of Fort Cottonwood. Two years later he built a ranch house along the Overland Trail south of North Platte and near what was later to be named Moran Canyon. During these same years he was also employed as an Indian interpreter and scout by the government.

In 1867, when Nebraska became a state, the wagon travel declined because of the completion of the railroad. Morin then began stock raising. Late in the summer of 1875 his wife, Valentine, was killed. An immigrant, excited at the sight of antelope, fired accidentally at her. Morin then moved to North Platte to be near his daughters. Having found his dawn just over the horizon, Morin died in 1902. He is buried in an unmarked grave in the North Platte Cemetery.

The two Frenchmen were influential on the plains and along the Platte River Valley not only as interpreters and scouts, but also in the promotion of the settlement in the area. History forbids us to know if their paths crossed before they both arrived in this area. Their lives were similiar ... two young boys seeking an adventurous and yet profitable life. Destiny brought them together at the same time in the same place, both with the same interests and tossed their families together albeit for a brief period of time.

Despite the fact that the early settlers in Lincoln County were French, credit goes usually to those of English origin. Anybody not of English ancestry was said to be *French*, regardless of his or her true nationality. The French were not considered white. Pallerdy and de Morin were two outstanding Frenchmen who came to the Platte River valley long before the English settlers described in the previous chapter. Historians fail to give them proper credit for their contributions.

CHAPTER 7

MILITARY ALONG THE PLATTE VALLEY

The population of Nebraska Territory in 1860 was 28,841. By the mid-1860s the only settlements which were established were located along the rivers Missouri, Platte and Little Blue.

The Indians of Nebraska during that same time period were grouped in nine tribes which spoke six different languages. They were the Missouri, the Sioux, the Pawnees, the Poncas, the Omahas, the Otoes, the Arapahoes, the Cheyennes, and the Winnebagoes. The Republican Pawnee Clan lived in the territory south of the Platte River to the Republican River. The southwestern portion of the state was held jointly by the Arapahoes and Southern Cheyennes. They carried on inter-tribal relations, with most of the battles being fought between the Pawnees and the allied Arapahoes and Cheyennes over possession of southwestern Nebraska. The Sioux also fought with the Pawnees.

Indian interpreter and trader, Washington Mallory Hinman, reported that one season there were 80 lodges of Indians near his residence in Shorter/Lincoln County. If they were Pawnee, as he eludes, their lodges were probably circular, earth structures consisting of a framework of four or more center poles with rafters. The rafters were covered with dirt and brush. There was an opening in the roof which served as a chimney. The Pawnees cultivated corn. Twice a year, they would abandon their villages for the buffalo hunts. During these hunts, the Indians lived in skin tipis. The highly skilled Pawnees, like their other Indian brothers, began to culturally decline as the white civilization progressed westward.

Fort Kearny was established in 1848 at the head of Grand Island, in Nebraska Territory. In 1849 Fort Laramie, in what is now Wyoming, was acquired by purchase from the American Fur Company. There were 300 miles of territory to be guarded between the posts.

Fortunately the Indians did not attack the settlers in Nebraska during the early sixties. Almost all of the troops had been withdrawn for service in the Civil War. During this time period there were 125 troops at Fort Kearny. There were 90 men stationed at Fort Laramie. George B. Grinnell in his book *THE FIGHTING CHEYENNES* stated that had the Indians wanted war during this time period they would have attacked, for at all times they knew the military strength at the various posts.

By mid 1863 there was an definite need for a military post between these two forts. On September 18, 1863 orders were issued by the Department of Nebraska directing that a detachment of Company G of the Seventh Iowa Volunteer Cavalry proceed to Cottonwood Springs and there erect a fort. The mouth of Cottonwood Canyon had been strategically selected for the fort as the Indians also used the area for a trail going north and south. Located just across the Platte River to the north were the Mormon Trail and California Trail.

The detachment, under the command of Lt. Eugene F. Ware, arrived at Cottonwood Springs on October 11, 1863. Temporary quarters were first established and then the actual building of permanent quarters ensued. The tall cedars in the canyons to the south were chopped, trimmed and snaked to the fort site. Lumber for the doors, window shutters and the furniture was "whip-sawed" on the site. By the time the first snow fell that winter, several buildings had been completed. This post was first named Cantonment McKean, but shortly it was changed to Post Cottonwood, then to Fort Cottonwood. Later the name was changed to Fort McPherson.

The fort was comprised of about 40 buildings which included stables, theater, commissary, hospital, bakery and band quarters. The roofs of the buildings were comprised of poles, cedar boughs and a ten-inch layer of hard packed clay. The clay was hauled up from the spring by wagon and used as chinking for the log walls and as plaster for the insides. The building were arranged around an open quadrangle or parade ground to obtain a stockade effect. Later a well was dug and a flag pole erected. The flag proudly flew in the middle of the parade ground.

During that winter of 1863 and 1864 the soldiers were kept busy with the policing the area, mounted drills and artillery practice. When the weather warmed more buildings were constructed. That same winter the traders at Cottonwood Springs and other stations in the area generally observed that the Cheyennes were no longer trading for guns and ammunition. The Cheyennes informed the traders that they had obtained guns and ammunition in Kansas and on the border of the Indian Territory.

In April 1864 several companies of the 11th Ohio Cavalry were ordered west to protect the Oregon Trail from Indian uprisings. The 11th Ohio Cavalry was partly composed of rebel prisoners who had taken the oath of allegiance and enlisted in the U.S. service. They were told that they would be used on the frontier to fight Indians. In the Union Army they were called "white washed rebs" and they called themselves "galvanized yanks."

Privates were paid approximately $16 a month out of which they had to pay for laundry and alteration services. Their weapons were furnished. They were charged $100 for a Spencer Carbine or $500 for a Colt if lost. After the first winter, women began to arrive. The officer's wives were allowed at the fort along with post laundresses. The latter lived on Soapsuds Alley. There was one laundress to each 19 enlisted men. It was said if a girl were pretty she usually got married after washing at the fort for about a week. If she was homely it took a whole month to get married.

The post was constructed none too soon as the Indian wars began in August of 1864. Large bands of Indians swarmed down upon the Platte and Little Blue Valleys, plundering the emigrant trains and stations. Settlers and emigrants were murdered and ranches destroyed. There were reports that in 1863 the Sioux, Cheyenne and Arapahoes had made an agreement to make war on the whites.

On April 17, 1864, June 8, 1864 and July 19, 1864 councils were held with the Brule and Ogallala Sioux at Cottonwood Springs. The military tried to secure a promise from the Indians that they would keep away from the Platte River Road. At the later meeting, General Mitchell brought along a company of Pawnee Indian Scouts in an attempt to make peace. No agreement was reached. After much arguing between the Pawnee and Sioux Chiefs, the Sioux were ordered to leave and not come back again.

On April 8, 1864 from Fort Leavenworth, Major S.S. Curtis communicated with Col. J.M. Chivington:

"I hear that Indians have committed depredations on or near Platte river.. Do not let District lines prevent pursuing and punishing them. Give Colonel Collins and General Mitchell your full co-operation and (all the) information you can. You can furlough veterans but give them government transportation."

The first council with the Indians was held at Fort Cottonwood on April 17, 1864. The Indians came in large numbers and camped about 2 miles west of the Fort. On the morning of April 17th, 100 warriors approached the fort on their best horses and in their greatest finery. Their visible arms were left with a guard, after which they dismounted and walked to the conference site. The army officers also put down their arms.

Their meeting was held in a building within the compound where the Indians squatted on one side while the officers sat opposite facing them. The Indians produced their "Peace Pipe" which was lighted and passed around the room. After it was used by all the Indians present it was passed to the soldiers.

The Sioux tribes were represented ... the Ogallallah by Chief Bad Wound; the Minneconjous from the northeast; the Brules under Shantag-a-lisk or Spotted Tail. Other chiefs present were Two Strike, Two Crows, The Big Mandan, Prickley Pear, and Eagle Twice.

General Mitchell through an interpreter asked that the Indians stay out of the Platte Valley. The Big Mandan rose and recalled how the Indians had been pushed westward. The whites were told of the Indian's plight and hunger. They were reminded that the government gave them food and that they should live like whites. The Indians in turn were only to hunt to the edge of the hills. In order to cross the Platte River they would need a military escort.

Spotted Tail stated that there was no hunting left in the valley, but they wanted to continue trading there. The Platte Valley belonged to the Indians and was used as a road only with the Indian's permission. Spotted Tail firmly stated that the Smoky Hill Road to the south must be closed and the military expedition to the Niobrara had to cease. The best buffalo hunting was south of the Platte and around the Smoky Hill River. Spotted Tail promised to match the whites warrior for warrior.

The Indians were fed molasses, bread and beef and then engaged in a feast of fat puppy. It would seem that from that moment on their thoughts concentrated not on peace, but on war.

On May 21, 1864 Major George M. O'Brien of Fort Cottonwood, sent the following message to Major C.S. Charlot, Asst. Adj-Gen. Dept. of Kansas:

"Have received the following from operator at Plum Creek. 'Major O'Brien. The Indians on Box Elder Creek, 175 miles southeast of here, have killed and butchered 10 soldiers. They say they will kill all white men and soldiers on the road. There are 1,640 warriors; will be here in twenty-four hours. They are the Cheyennes. We have just come in from them, and they say they will strike the road near French's road. Cinnamond-Operator.' Indian troubles are much magnified. I see nothing to cause serious alarm here, and this point is considered the most central."

Major H.D. Walen of the Seventh Infantry sent this message to the Adjudant General on June 20, 1864:

"I have just crossed the plains and am sure from authentic information that an expensive Indian War is about to take place between the whites and the Cheyennes, Kiowas, and a band of Araphaoes. It can be prevented by prompt management."

The Inspector General, Major T.K. McKenny, reported:

"I think if great caution is not exercised on our part there will be a bloody war. It should be our policy to try and conciliate them ... and stop these scouting parties that are roaming over the country that do not know one tribe from another, and who will kill anything in the shape of an Indian. It will require but few murders on the part of our troops to unite all these warlike tribes of the plains, who have been at peace for year."

On June 19, 1864 Brigadier-General Robert B. Mitchell relayed information on the June 8, 1864 council with the Indians held at Cottonwood Springs. The papers were forwarded to Major C.S. Charlot by Major George M. O'Brien.

Inclosure No. 1
Headquarters.
Fort Cottonwood, Nebr. Ter.
June 8, 1864

In pursuance (of) an invitation from these headquarters, dated May 31, 1864, the following Indian chiefs reported with their braves, to hold a council: O-A-Sehu-Cha or Bad Wound, Con-qu-num-pa or Two Crows, Zo-lah or Whistler, Cur-tig-a-lisha or Spotted Tail, Two Strike, Long Face. Little Thunder authorized Spotted Tail to represent him in council, as he was sick and unable to attend.

By Major Commanding.

Question. Do you propose to remain peaceable?

Answer. We have been peaceable since our treaty, and want to remain so. We will not fight with our white brothers.

Question. In case you had to fight, which side would you take, Cheyenne or White?

Answer. We cannot be forced to fight on either side; we do not want to fight the Cheyennes, and will not fight the whites, as the whites could kill all of us. We want to be permitted to live and hunt our game where we can find it, as was stipulated with us in treaty, and in so doing (remaining quiet and hunting) we want protection from our white brethren, as they are more numerous than we are.

The Commander. Then, as you appear to want to remain peaceable, you must keep your people off the Platte Valley road, and not allow them to interfere with emigrants, nor trade with them, but you may visit the road in small numbers and trade for clothing and provisions. You must not remain long on the road in so trading. Also, you must not interfere with stock belonging to white people, in any way. Some of your people have been in the habit of trading for whiskey, indirectly. This I insist on having stopped, and in case any white man offers to sell, or trade you whiskey, either directly or indirectly, I require you, the chiefs and headmen, to report such immediately to these headquarters. Also during this war with the Cheyennes you must not get up any war parties against the Pawnees, as it will have a tendency to get you into war with the whites. You are also required to report to these headquarters any hostile movement in the direction of the Platte Valley road, or otherwise, coming with your knowledge.

If you agree with these instructions, I want it distinctly understood that in case you fail to comply with them you will be considered as enemies, like the Cheyennes, and treated accordingly; but if you comply you will be considered friends.

Reply. We agree to all, but want assurance that when you send out soldiers against the Cheyennes that we won't be molested. We are afraid your soldiers will not know us and may take us for hostile Indians and kill us. We also want to be allowed to remain on the South side of the Platte river to hunt our game. We cannot live without game, and there is none in the country north of the Platte, where we are allowed to hunt. We also want a white man with us to show you we intend to do as we agreed, and in order to prevent us from being attacked by your soldiers, not knowing us. We now are gathering all our people together and will not allow any of them to scatter until this war is over between the whites and the Cheyennes. There are some of our young men among the Cheyennes, but we ordered them home. All have now come, except 6 women who are married to Cheyenne men. We have now together 210 lodges and expect some more. We want to be told from time to time what is wanted us to do. We want our goods distributed to us on the north side of the Platte about ten miles above this point, as we are so poor and our horses so few we cannot go to Fort Laramie to receive them. It would not pay us for our trouble, and if we do not go we are afraid you and our white brothers will think we mean to be hostile, which is not the case.

The Commander: I cannot give you any assurance that your goods will be distributed where you want them, but will recommend it be done this time; however, you must not think it will be done because I say I will recommend it. The Government wants to do what is best for you; they (Indians understand Government to mean white people acting together as one man) want you to live peaceably among yourselves and with your white brothers. Occasionally you will find foolish and bad white men that may want to make trouble with you. Do not mind them, but report them to these headquarters and they will be punished. I also want to warn you that any of your people found committing any depredation will also be punished, and should you fail to give such as commit any crime up to us when demanded you will be treated as enemies and punished as white men have been accustomed to punish you, for instance, as Harney treated you.

Reply. We have said all we want to know is what to do and we would do it. We will do as you have said you want us. We have some robes and pelties that we want to trade for food and clothes, and want traders allowed to go to our village, situated south of Plum Creek. Our Agent, Major Lord, would not let any but one man trade with us, and that man had only a little goods for so many Indians, so we are bad off for many things; we were afraid to come on the road, as we heard you would kill us, so we now have more to trade than we want to bring on the road and want traders.

The Commander. I have no objections for a few good men to go trade with you, providing I can be satisfied that these man will not trade you whiskey.

Question, by the Commander.
State what you know about the Cheyennes.

Answer.

Cheyennes, Arapahoes, Kiowas and Comanches had a fight with soldiers on Island Wood Creek; killed two officers and one soldier, and wounded two more that since died. Cheyennes lost two chiefs and one brave. Soldiers fought two days, then went south (fighting as they go) to Fort Lyon. There may have been more Indians. Cheyennes have killed two ranchmen on the Santa Fe road, and say they will kill all the whites on both the Platte Valley and Santa Fe roads, and we believe they will try to do so. They will fight as long as they can, then go south to the Arkansas River and escape.

Question. What do you think of the Cheyennes in making war on the whites?

Answer. We think they are fools, and will all be killed.

Question. Have you any more to say? I am done.

Answer. We are happy and glad to meet you and shake hands with your white brothers in token of friendship, to show them that our hearts are good. We wanted to come and see you long ago, but were afraid. When we got your inviation we were all glad. Our wives and children and head men all cried for joy. So now we all shake hands with you as a token of our friendship and good feeling.

(Here all shake hands, and after that, smoke.)

The above is the substance of the conversation. There was much unimportant talk not deemed essential.

Washington M. Hinman
Indian Interpreter

On June 26, 1864 at Omaha, John Pratt, A.A.G. by command of General Mitchell sent a message to Major George M. O'Brien of Cottonwood Springs ...

"Have a gun squad organized from your dismounted men under command of Capt. O'Brien. There are four mountain howitzers here. They will be sent west tomorrow."

July 19, 1864 from Fort Cottonwood, General Mitchell contacted Major General Curtis ...

"Can I have your permission to raise 200 100-days' men from the ranchmen along this line? They all understand the Indian character and the country, and are accustomed to fighting Indians. I can raise them in ten days, and have them in the field with their own horses and arms. Reply at Julesburg."

In reply, Major General S.R. Curtis, on July 20, 1864 at Fort Leavenworth ...

"Governor's call for militia would be more speedy and proper. I have no authority for such a call. Order Collins with most of his force down to Fremont's Orchard and Camp Collins. Make the Overland Stage Route as secure as possible. Confer with Governor Evans, who ought to move his militia in the same way. Direct all your cavalry to be armed, and horses or no horses, let them move up to take care of posts. Stop any trains that seem to be going into danger. Keep me informed as to your movements and the facts relating to the Indians."

On August 7, 1864 the Indians made their first attack at Plum Creek on the Overland Route. The site of this was a half mile east of Plum Creek station, which was located on the Platte River Road about a mile west of the mouth of Plum Creek and 35 miles west of Fort Kearny; now in the northwest corner of Phelps County. The following day every stage station and ranch between Fort Kearny and Julesburg was attacked and many destroyed. Telegraphed messages to all the stations along the line saved many lives. Many of the settlers took shelter at Fort Cottonwood. Between Fort Cottonwood and Plum Creek many were killed an scalped.

A few miles east of Cottonwood Springs, at the Gillette Ranch, the two Gillette brothers were killed. Their father was scalped. A settler working in a hay field near the fort was killed and at the Gilman Ranch three men were killed. Their bodies were badly mutilated and shot full of arrows.

After this August 1864 raid the area along the Platte river changed. The Indians retired to their camps and there was a general state of panic on the Nebraska frontier. From Omaha to the mountains in

Colorado Territory there was terror. Many of the settlers began to flee eastward. The Overland Route was completely closed by the Indians for over a month. Mail going to Denver had to sent to Panama, across the Isthmus and up the Pacific coast. From San Francisco it came inland by Overland stage to Denver.

On August 12, 1864, at Cottonwood, General Mitchell sent the following message to Major General Curtis ...

"Am I to have any aid in horses or men in this distrcit? I have 600 miles of country invaded by Indians, all within four days. Yesterday there was another attack on the road near Laramie. From the South Pass to within forty miles of Nebraska City there have been constant raids on the road for four days, and for three weeks the same thing has been done from Fort Laramie to South Pass. I am concentrating at strong points along the road all citizens and trains for their own protection. The citizens are generally without effective weapons. I have positive proof that there are white men, guerillas, in large numbers aiding the Indians against us. I have ordered horses bought."

Four days later General Mitchell dispatched the following from Fort Kearny to Major General Curtis at Omaha ...

"Your dispatch is received. The amount of damage done west of here is hard to estimate. There have been twenty persons killed between here and Cottonwood and one train burnt. The ranchmen have all left, except where we have posts occupied by the military, from Cottonwood and Julesburg. The ranchmen have all run except two posts occupied by the military. The stage stock has been taken off today, I am informed by the agent from Julesburg to Cottonwood. Unless the government intends to abandon the Laramie Route entirely, I have taken all the troops off that route that can possibly be spared. I have taken from that route two companies of the Eleventh Ohio Cavalry, one stationed at Fremont's Orchard, the other at Camp Collins, extending two posts toward Julesburg. I have made the headqaurters of one company Seventh Iowa Cavalry at Julesburg, one post extending each way. We occupy the road west from Collins to South Pass. My troops are just scattered enough to be cut up by details. Captain Murphy, Seventh Iowa Cavalry, has been on the Blue since last Thursday with his company. Have heard nothing from him since he left Pawnee Ranch. Major O'Brien reports a skirmish between his troops and Cheyennes today at six miles east of Cottonwood. I will probably start for Omaha tomorrow for the purpose of conferring with you."

During the month of September in 1864, some men were working at or near the Hinman place when they were surprised by Indians and killed. In October of 1864 Mrs. Charles McDonald was returning form a visit in Omaha when she narrowly escaped attack. She had been waiting at Fort Kearny for a safe time to return to Cottonwood Springs. She took a special stage coach and arrived safely in the night. The regular stage with several military officers on board came a few hours later. That stage was attacked by Indians within a short distance of Fort Cottonwood. The Indians were beaten back and only one on board was slightly wounded.

General Curtis with a small force, left Fort Leavenworth to investigate the hostilities along the Platte River. He was joined by Brigadier General Mitchell at Fort Kearny. After reaching the forks of the Solomon River on September 7th, the command divided with General Curtis and detachment going east and General Mitchell and detachment going west. Mitchell sent out scouting parties to look for the Indians at their favorite camping grounds. On September 17th they reached Cottonwood Springs on the Platte River and two days later moved up the North Platte River in hopes of finding a band of Brule Sioux there. At the old California crossing they met a small band of Ogalala Sioux under the leadership of Two Face. The Indians were friendly and were sent by General Mitchell to Fort Cottonwood for protection. The Indians were always ahead of Mitchell and his detachment. From the headwaters of the Loup forks and Niobrara Rivers in the sand hills, Mitchell marched the troops down the river, arriving at Cottonwood Springs on September 24, 1864. They had traveled 200 miles and had seen no hostile Indians.

On September 25, 1864, Sepcial Field Orders No. 22 were issued from Hdqrs. District of Nebraska, Post Cottonwood, In the Field, by John K. Rankin, Lieut. and Aide-de-Camp:

I. Major G.M. O'Brien, Seventh Iowa Cavalry is relieved from command of Post Cottonwood, and will turn over to Colonel S.W. Summers all public property in his possession.

II. Colonel S.W. Summers, Seventh Iowa Cavalry, will immediately assume command of Post Cottonwood, receipting to Major G.M. O'Brien for all public property belonging to the post.

By Command of R.B. Mitchell, Brigadier-General, commanding.

On October 31, 1864 the following units were stationed in the area:

Post Cottonwood, Nebraska Territory
7th Iowa Cavalry (detachment) Lt. Harrison W. Cremer Co. C
1st Battalion Nebraska Cavalry Company C, Capt. Henry Kuhl

Gillman's Station
1st Battalion, Nebraska Cavalry Company A (detachment)
Capt. Charles F. Porter

Mullahla's Station, Nebraska Territory
1st Nebraska Cavalry, Company B, Lt. Morgan A. Hance
1st Nebraska Cavalry, Company I, Capt. Henry H. Ribble

O'Fallon's Bluffs, Nebraska Territory
7th Iowa Cavalry, Co. B, Capt. John Wilcox

In a desperate message dated November 10, 1864, to Major General Curtis at Fort Leavenworth, General Mitchell relayed information on the conditions ...

"My men are in a starving condition at Kearny, Plum Creek, Cottonwood, O'Fallon's Bluff, Alkali and Julesburg. All estimates have been forwarded for two or three months and no attention has been paid to them at department headquarters. If they cannot be supplied the necessary result will be starvation or desertion. We have pressed teams and sent everything we have here to them to do for a few days."

In the fall of 1864 there were no actual raids. There were also not enough soldiers to send out an expedition against the camps of hostile Cheyennes and Sioux. Sometimes the Indians would make a raid in late afternoon. If the soldiers followed them, darkness would prevent a conflict. These night raids resulted in the following order from Colonel Livingston to William Reynolds, General Superintendent of the Overland Stage Lines, on November 27, 1864:

"In view of the frequent ambuscades by hostile Indians between this post (Fort Kearny) and Fort Cottonwood, and the fact that nearly all these hostile demonstrations occur after darkness, I deem it essential to the safety of the U.S. Mail and the lives of the passengers in your coaches that you make it incumbent on your division agent to run the coaches between this post and Fort Cottonwood by daylight. I respectfully suggest the hour of four A.M. as a seasonable hour for departure of the coach from this point for the west, and three A.M. for the departure of the coach going eastward from Cottonwood."

In the fall of 1864 scurvy had broken out at the Fort. The post hospital did not have supplies to cope with the disease so the staff doctor recommended that the soldiers obtain as much fruit as possible. The morning of September 20, 1864, a Captain Mitchell, along with Corporal Anderson and an orderly, loaded up seven patients in an ambulance and drove south into Cottonwood Canyon. Plum thickets filled with ripe fruit grew in abundance throughout the canyon. They went to a point about 7 miles from the post where they were met by two troopers who had been detailed to locate some stray mules. They, too, were picking the wild fruit.

The soldiers felt secure as the Indians had not been seen for sometime. Suddenly there was a crack of rifles and a few Indians were seen coming from some nearby bushes, firing at the soldiers. The patients climbed into the canvas covered ambulance and with the officers started at a full gallop down the canyon. The two troopers mounted and began to retreat. One of them on a mule was badly wounded and later killed. A band of warriors soon approached the ambulance. Captain Mitchell ordered the driver to drive up the side of the canyon wall toward the tableland and then head for the post.

As this then seemed impossible, Captain Mitchell shouted for the ambulance to halt so they could make a stand. The driver made no effort to restrain his team. As Corporal Anderson went to take the lines, he fell from the wagon. Captain Mitchell then jumped to put on the brakes, but was pitched headlong into a gully. The Indians did not see the two men fall from the wagon. Anderson had held on to his rifle and Mitchell had two revolvers. Nine Indians were killed before Anderson was wounded and captured. The trooper's body was mutilated. The ambulance was overtaken and all the soldiers were killed.

The Indians picked up their dead and headed south toward the Republican Valley. Having been in hiding in the bushes, Captain Mitchell reached the Fort late that night. The tragedy became known as the *Cottonwood Massacre.*

Another account of the massacre is contained in an Army report from Lieutenant Thomas Flangan. He reported that while the soldiers were three miles from the post they were attacked by a party of 60-70 Indians. Four of the troopers were killed and the others escaped to the Fort.

Under Special Orders No. 122 General Mitchell detailed the boundary of Cottonwood Springs on November 29, 1864.

"Cottonwood Springs, Nebr. Ter.: Commencing at the flag-staff in the center of the parade ground at that post, thence east three miles, thence north three miles, thence west six miles, thence south three miles, thence west twelve miles, thence south fifteen miles, thence east thirty miles, thence north fifteen miles, thence west twelve miles to a point three miles east of the place of beginning."

During the history of the fort there were three field campaigns by large numbers of troops which were considered of great importance. The campaigns were: General Mitchell's expedition against the Indians in the Republican country in 1865, the Republican expedition in 1866 and the Battle of Summit Springs in the northeast corner of the present state of Colorado in 1869.

In January of 1865 General Mitchell set about organizing a command at Fort Cottonwood to strike the Indians in that section. He was to lead an expedition to keep the Indians on the move so they would be unable to organize. Two companies from Fort Cottonwood comprised the troops. They departed the fort on January 16, 1865, marching in a southwest direction down what was called *Trader's Trail*. This particular trail followed a canyon running from the fort to a point south of the present city of North Platte.

From there the expedition continued southwesterly until they reached the Kansas-Nebraska border and from there 50 miles into Kansas. They then turned toward the Republican River and followed that stream eastward as far as the mouth of the Medicine Creek, then turned north to Fort Cottonwood. They reached the fort on January 26, 1865.

There was great suffering on this expedition. At one time the temperature reached -20 degrees. There was nothing more than pup tents for shelter and on several nights the troops sat around the fire to avoid freezing to death. From morning until night they searched for hostile Indians. The only ones they saw were lone Indians probably scouting for the main body. They discovered Indian trails, but returned to Fort Cottonwood in failure.

A message on January 25, 1865, from Jno. Pratt Assistant Adjudant General at Omaha to Major C.S. Charlot at Fort Leavenworth ...

"General Mitchell left the road at Morrow's Ranch on the 18th instant going southeast with expedition. Having had no communciation with him since that date. On the 19th Indians drove off 300 head of cattle near Alkali. Indians, estimated from 70 to 100 lodges, crossed the Platte going north."

General Mitchell considered this failure to locate Indians a reflection on his ability as a frontier soldier and suffered mental depression. He resolved that the Indians would be punished for their depredations even if he could not do battle with them.

On the morning of January 27, 1865, General Mitchell cleared the telegraph lines and wired all military commanders from Fort Kearny to Denver to set the prairie on fire that evening at sundown. His idea of burning the prairie was to force the Indians to leave that part of the country for the winter.

By the evening of January 27, 1865, the entire 300 miles was ablaze. The wind took care of the rest. Even the expectations of General Mithcell were exceeded as three days later it was still burning along the banks of the Arkansas River and down into the panhandle of Texas.

In February of 1865, General Dodge at Fort Leavenworth reported to General Mitchell in Omaha that 100 teams had left Fort Leavenworth a week hence for Denver. Reportedly 75 of them were to unload at Cottonwood; the wagons to go through to Denver empty. The following week 150 teams were to haul for Cottonwood and Julesburg.

The following communication undoubtedly touched the lives of all the officers and soldiers at Fort Cottonwood and elsewhere:

Headquarters Department of the Missouri
April 15, 1865, 1:40 p.m.

Brigadier-General Connor.   Denver

President Lincoln and Secretary Seward were assassinated last night; Mr. Lincoln while attending the theater; said to be done by J. Wilkes Booth; Mr. Seward at his home. Mr. Lincoln died this a.m. by 7:30. Mr. Seward at 9:30. A general gloom overspreads the community.

G.M. Dodge, Major-General

A report of mid-summer 1865 shows that there were approximately 1,250 men stationed at Fort Cottonwood. Large amounts of stores were taken from there to Laramie to fit out General Conner's expedition, contractors having failed to deliver supplies in time.

Major George M. O'Brien of the Seventh Iowa Cavalry, commander of Post Cottonwood in 1865 reported in June of that year a list of stage stations between Fort Kearny, Nebraska Territory and Julesburg, Colorado Territory. The following are shown for Lincoln County and are noted that they were garrisoned by troops from Post (Fort) Cottonwood:

Dan Smith's Station to Gillman's Station - 10 miles
Gillman's Station to Dan Trout's Station - 12 miles
Dan Trout's Station to Post Cottonwood - 4 miles
Post Cottonwood to Box Elder Station - 3 miles
Box Elder Station to Jack Morrow's Station - 10 miles
Jack Morrow's Station to Bishop's Station - 10 miles
Bishop's Station to Fremont Springs Station - 10 miles
Fremont Springs Station to O'Fallon's Bluffs Station - 2 miles
O'Fallon's Bluffs Station to Elkhorn Station - 10 miles

Also in June of 1865 Major-General G.M. Dodge reported to Brig. General Connor, Commander of the District of the Platte, that there were rations at Cottonwood for 1,200 men for one year. For one year he reported there were 1,175 cavalry and 800 infantry at Cottonwood.

The following month Brig.-General Conner reported from Fort Laramie to Major-General Dodge ...

"Part of the First Nebraska Cavalry stationed at Kearny claim, as the war is over, that they are entitled to discharge, and have mutinied. I have ordered Colonel Heath to suppress it with grape and mutinied. I have ordered Colonel Heath to suppress it with grape and canister, and bring the leaders to trial. I will have subsistence sufficient from Kearny and Cottonwood in four days to move the column. There is ony one contractors train this side of Julesburg; it is loaded with bacon only, and was diverted from Denver. The Indians are still very troublesome, and are scattered in small bands along the mail and telegraph lines; their families are north. I hear of a large body of Indians on the Heart River. I shall make my arrangements to continue the campaign during the winter, if necessary. I can hear nothing of the mowing machines ordered for Powder River. I hope the troops from Leavenworth will move as rapidly as possible. I have no troops enough, and should have some more whose time does not expire this fall. I have great confidence in being able to close the war before midwinter. I am losing much precious time now; cause contractirs(sic)."

In January and February of 1866 an expedition marched from the fort south toward the Indians in the Republican country. The "Post Returns" for January 1866, show that the troops were in the field about a month, with the returns for February stating that they had returned. It was a large expedition as the roster shows the 1st Nebraska Veteran Cavalry, Companies, A, E, I and C; 7th Iowa Volunteer Cavalry, Companies A, B, G and H; and the 12th Missouri Volunteer Cavalry, Company C comprised the expedition. Once again this expedition failed to defeat any great number of Indians.

A diary left by John B. Patterson of Company B, 7th Iowa Volunteer Cavalry, relates that about 700 men left Fort Cottonwood and marched 25 miles to Medicine Creek. They marched about 25 miles per day until January 16, 1866. On that date they engaged in a fight with Indians on the Sappa Creek in northwest Kansas. They received orders to return to the fort on January 18, 1866. The march back was begun on January 30, 1866, at the rate of one to 25 miles per day. They were attacked by about 100 Indians on February 16, 1866 and returned to the fort on February 19, 1866.

As is evidenced from the military communications, there were troops stationed at various locations along the Overland Trail. One little-known fort was located near the present day community of Sutherland in Lincoln County. It was known as Fort Heath. Documents show that it was occupied as early as 1866 and as late as 1870.

In January of 1867, slightly before the naming of Nebraska as a state, the city of North Platte was in planning stages. Company I, 36th

Infantry was sent from Fort McPherson to develop a station or post at North Platte. The commanding officer was Capt. Arthur MacArthur, the father of General Douglas MacArthur of World War I and II.

The troops encamped first just north of the railroad tracks and lived in tents during that cold winter. By spring they were dispatched to Fort Sedgwick, Colorado. By the fall of 1867 they had returned and moved 400 yards west of the railroad depot and 200 feet south of the tracks to a townsite owned by the Union Pacific Railroad. For a brief period of time this encampment was known as Camp Sargent, but later became officially North Platte Station. This post remained useful for 11 years, closing in January of 1878.

In a monthly report issued from Fort Cottonwood on January 20, 1866 the name of the fort was changed to Fort McPherson. This was confirmed by General Order No. 19, Department of Missouri, dated February 26, 1866. The name was changed to honor Major-General James B. McPherson who had been killed in action on July 22, 1864, while commanding the Army of the Tennessee at the Battle of Atlanta.

Because of the numerous deaths due to skirmishes, disease and other causes, a cemetery was started on a hill near Fort Cottonwood. On March 3, 1873, a 107 acre tract near Fort McPherson was designated as a national cemetery. Graves were moved from the original cemetery. The identities of those buried there were generally unknown. The roster of the dead for Fort McPherson National Cemetery as well as the identical white markers show only a number. In those evenly spaced rows there are over 500 unknown dead.

Julius Birge wrote in 1866 ..."On the evening of June 22 our national flag was seen in the west, streaming out from the staff at Fort McPherson."

The flag ceased to fly at Fort McPherson when Special Order No. 26, Department of the Platte was issued March 25, 1880. At that time the fort was declared surplus and to be abandoned and decommissioned in April of 1880. An era in the history of the Platte Valley was coming to an end. As silent and constant as the unmarked graves of those who had traversed the Platte Valley, the flag still flies nearby at the Fort McPherson National Cemetery.

CHAPTER 8

RAILS TO NORTH PLATTE

The rolling, clanking wagon wheels of the immigrant wagons and stage coaches were replaced by steel wheels. The Platte Valley Road was destined to never be the same.

Primarily because of the need for a faster route to the Pacific, talk began as early as 1836 about the construction of a railroad. It was debated by Congress after the Fremont explorations in 1842 and 1846. In 1853 Senator Salmon P. Chase introduced a bill for appropriations to explore routes to the Pacific. Because of the geography of the country, all routes tended to be expensive. None followed the present lines of the railroads.

Entrepreneur Thomas Durant hoped to extend the Missisippi and Missouri Railroad to the Pacific coast. This line was being built across Iowa. He sent his engineer, Grenville M. Dodge, to make surveys and collect data.

Economically the timing was poor as the panic of 1857 stopped everything. Dodge was caught up in this in Council Bluffs, Iowa, then a tiny settlement. The next obstacle was the Civil War which eliminated any southern route to the Pacific. It was then that the obvious route for the railroad became apparent ... the Platte Valley road westward. This accessible route had been followed for centuries by buffalo, Indians, explorers, traders and immigrants.

At the same time it became apparent that if the railroad route was to be constructed the government would have to do the financing. Several promotion companies began vying for the contract. The Pacific Railroad Act was passed on July 1, 1862. This provided for a hundred million dollar corporation, which was the largest capitalization ever known in the United States. It presented promoters with a right of way through the public lands, 200 feet each side, for the entire distance; the free use of building materials from the public lands; the annulment of Indian titles; every alternate odd numbered section of public land to the amount of 4 sections a mile on each side; a subsidy of $16,000 a mile on the plains and from $32,000 to $48,000 a mile through the mountains.

Ground was broken on December 2, 1863 near the ferry landing on the west bank of the Missouri River at Omaha. With great ceremony, prayers of blessing, messages of congratulations and a grand banquet, the railroad pushed westward slowly. By the spring of 1866, only 60 miles of rails had been laid.

That spring General Grenville M. Dodge, of the Union Army, was called back to become Chief Engineer of the railroad. Dodge had the capability and knowledge to see the project through. Survey parties were kept working ahead of the rails. These consisted of 18 to 22 men, well armed and usually with military escort. They were working in hostile Indian country and were often under attack. By the summer of 1866 the tracks had been laid to Kearney and trains were running to that destination.

In addition to the Indian hostilities, the railroad construction workers had to contend with hauling in materials from Omaha, much of which had been freighted up the Missouri River. Across treeless Nebraska the tracks were laid. Trees were brought into Omaha for shipment westward. Any kind was accepted ... oak, cedar, even cottonwood. Thomas Durant proceeded to make the poor cottonwood acceptable for tracks. He set up an iron boiler 100 feet long and 5 feet in diameter. Filling it with the cottonwood ties he closed it tightly, exhausted the air with a steam engine and injected a solution of zinc. This permeated the fibers of the wood and dried it, giving guaranteed durability for years. It is estimated that 2,500 ties were laid to a mile, with extras for sidings.

There were some trees on the plains of Nebraska. These were in the canyons south of the Platte River in Lincoln County. Fortunes were made by men like John Burke and Jack Morrow, who cut and hauled ties from the canyon hills north to the railroad construction sites.

On October 6, 1866 the track crossed the 100th meridian near present Cozad, 247 miles from Omaha. Just after the excursion celebrating this, Dodge went to the projected site of North Platte to select the station grounds. It was to be a railroad division point 291 miles from Omaha at the junction of the North and South Platte rivers. He described it as follows:

"I selected a large acerage for the station, division station, and sidings for the future. I went on the principle that it was best to take all the property needed or that ever would be needed while the land was vacant, and that policy has been of the greatest benefit to the Union Pacific Railroad Company, for the large number of acres, at some of its points 160 to 640 acres of lands, which were selected at that time is still held today and is of great value to the property."

On December 3, 1866 the Union Pacific Railroad reached North Platte. It crossed the river by a cedar pile trestle bridge 2,300 feet long. That winter the construction continued 14 miles further west to near O'Fallons Bluffs, before stopping. The railroad had reached 305 miles west of Omaha. North Platte became the first of the notorious "Hell-on-Wheels" towns, an expression credited to Samuel Bowles, editor of the Springfield (Mass.) *Republican*.

During a nine month period of time from April to December 1866, 265 miles of track had been laid. That was more than had ever been built anywhere. The Casements averaged 1 3/4 miles per day for the days worked and sometimes reached 3 miles per day. Two days after the tracks had been laid down, cars moved over them smoothly at 30 to 40 miles per hour. Dodge wrote that it was a "first-class American road."

The contract for constructing the previously mentioned railroad bridge was assigned in 1866 to a man by the name of Gessner. For sometime it was referred to as the Gessner Bridge. The piling was native red cedar, mostly secured from Moran Canyon at the price of $15 each. The pilings were cut by Tom Welch who had a ranch at Fort McPherson and was known as a "horse doctor."

One morning while eating breakfast with his assistants in Moran Canyon, Welch's camp was invaded by six Indians armed with rifles. From the belt of one hung the scalp of the man who had been guarding the camp horses. The Indians bound all the men in the camp and began ransacking it.

Chief Sleepy Eyes was in the group of Indians and while the other warriors drank horse liniment, he ate sugar. When the other Indians became very ill, Chief Sleepy Eyes demanded that Welch cure them. He administered an antidote. Consequently Chief Sleepy Eyes made peace with the white men. Every morning thereafter he would appear with squaws who assited in felling the trees.

In late December 1866, General J.H. Simpson passed through this area on an inspection tour and noted that where there had once been prairie three weeks earlier there now stood about 20 buildings, including a brick roundhouse capable of storing 40 engines. Nearby was a frame depot and a frame hotel which cost $18,000. Within a few months North Platte claimed 15 business houses, nine of which served food and/or drink.

In January 1867 the Union Pacific attained a railroad connection with the East, when the Oakes' Cedar Rapids & Missouri River Railroad entered Council Bluffs. It was then that North Platte grew with construction workers, traders, miners, soldiers, teamsters, adventurers and speculators. The population reached 5,000, all within six months.

In the spring of 1867, Major Henry C. Parry, Dodge's medical officer, wrote:

"I found as I passed through North Platte that the Indians had driven all the traders and miners in from the mountains, and at North Platte they (the miners and traders) were having a good time, gambling, drinking, and shooting each other. There were fifteen houses in North Platte. One hotel, nine eating or drinking saloons, one billiard room, three groceries, and one engine house, belonging to the Pacific Railroad Company. The last named building is the finest structure in the station. I observed that in every establishment the persons behind the counters attended to their customers with loaded and half-cocked revolvers in their hands. Law is unknown here, and the people are about to get up a vigilance committee."

A gambling saloon in North Platte has been described as a rude structure made of logs and lumber, housing four card tables. Prominently displayed on the wall was a sign stating that disputes would be settled by the code of the West. An Irish resident of North Platte stated that "...North Platte is a town where people suffer for a time before going to hell."

As mentioned previously a company of soldiers was stationed at North Platte during the winter of 1866-1867, primarily to protect the construction crews. They lived in tents during this severe winter. One out of nine deserted, only to be captured and incarcerated. Life was reckless and far from comfortable in the early days of North Platte.

When the railroad was first operable in early 1867 from points east to North Platte, some of the first passengers were Indians. They were relatively peaceful that year, so were given free use of the trains. They were like children with a new toy, but required to ride the car platforms or on top of the cars. Once the entire line was completed coast to coast, travelers paid $325 for first class facilities. It took seven days and nights to traverse the continent.

William S. Peniston was eulogized by the *Evening Telegraph* in October of 1906 as being North Platte's first merchant and first citizen. He was born in Peniston, Yorkshire, England in 1834 and as a child emigrated with his parents to Quebec, Canada. He came to Nebraska Territory in 1859, an adventerous 25 year old. Peniston first settled in Nebraska City and in 1860 with A.J. Miller established a store and half-way house along the Overland Trail at Cold Water on Willow Island. This was located 25 miles west of Plum Creek, now Lexington.

During the Indian wars of 1864, they were forced to flee for their lives. In 1865, Will Penniston married Anna Webb in Auburn, New York. On the same day, his partner, A.J. Miller, married Anna's cousin. Anna's sister married Dr. F.H. Dick, who would become North Platte's first physician, excluding those at the military posts of Fort McPherson and Camp North Platte or North Platte Station.

Immediately after their marriages, the Penistons and Millers came west to the store at Cold Water. The Union Pacific reached there in the summer of 1866. Miller, while on a trip to Omaha, learned that North Platte was to be the railroad division point. He and Peniston quickly decided it would be to their advantage to locate their business there. Lumber and building materials were brought from Denver and hauled to the newly-platted North Platte site by the railroad company. The Penistons and Millers camped there in September of 1866 then selected and purchased a lot for their store.

The store was located on what is now the corner of Front and Jeffers. The frame building was actually the first building in North Platte, open for business on November 8, 1866. They prospered, selling to the railroad workers, camp followers as well as travelers by rail and wagon, and Indians.

Early in 1867 they moved the log store from Cold Water to North Platte. The building was sold along with half of the lot to Althimer & Co. for $1,111. The building was dismantled and set up for the railroad construction crews as they progressed westward.

Peniston's newspaper obituary credits him with persuading the railroad company to keep the North Platte townsite where it remains today, instead of moving it a few miles to the west.

The Peniston and Miller partnership was dissolved in 1870. Shortly before this an ad was placed in the *North Platte Republican* newspaper which read:

"Peniston and Miller. Wholesale and Retail Dealers in Dry Goods. Groceries, Provisions, Clothing, Grain, Hardware, Tinware, Liquors, Robes, Boots, Shoes and in fact everything usually kept in a general store. We respectfully ask our share of patronage of the public. Our Motto: WE WILL NOT BE UNDERSOLD."

Miller continued in the log store until 1872 when he sold the building to Charles McDonald and the stock to Otto Uhling. Peniston became interested in government. In the early 1870s he was county treasurer for two years, a justice of the peace and county judge for two or three terms. He served as United States Commissioner for over 30 years. Many persons who committed federal crimes were brought before him for preliminary hearings. For 25 years he was employed "more or less" as clerk in the U.S. land office. He also served seven terms in the Nebraska Territorial legislature.

The second building in North Platte was a log structure moved from Cottonwood Springs by John Burke. It was used as a hotel. The first lawyers in North Platte were P.B. Enos and Beach I. Hinman who arrived in about November of 1866. There were not many lawsuits so they made loans, paid taxes for eastern parties and insured property. The first post office was established in 1867 and William Healy was the first postmaster.

The town did not officially become organized until December 28, 1875. It was known by a variety of names from "Platte City" to "North Platte City" to just "North Platte." The early newspaper in North Platte was called *The Pioneer on Wheels*. The press rolled into town on a boxcar and was set off on a siding. In 1867 it rolled on to Julesburg, following the construction of the railroad line. Just as quickly as the population had increased overnight with the coming of the railroad to North Platte, so it decreased. By 1867 figures show that the population was estimated at 150. North Platte would survive and grow. While many of its would-be citizens moved west with the railroad construction, some remained to live out their lives in this division point of the railroad.

On March 1, 1867 Nebraska changed from a Territory to a State. A governmental act on paper, a change of great magnitude, but the passing of the old territory probably created little concern to the citizens of Lincoln County.

A contract for $850 per mile of track laying had been signed and on March 7, 1867 Dodge wired to open work on the fourth hundred miles and have it graded by May 1, 1867. It was business as usual.

Through the years, the Platte Valley had resounded with the rhythmic beat of the soldier's trod and echoed with the percussion of the immigrant trains. They were all there ... the immigrants, the soldiers, the railroad tycoons, the traders and trappers, the ranchers, the Indians, the squawmen and the squaws, the pretty ladies, the stage coach drivers, the herdsmen and those who had the confidence to remain.

Like a prowling, invading wind, the white man had preyed upon the land. Easing his way onto it, then gusting forth with excitement, fervor and reverberating with of lust for adventure, wealth and fame, he made his final claim. Like the whispering, gentle breeze, the native Indian retreated. The serenity of the endless, treeless miles of grass and sand in the Platte Valley had been interrupted by the churning wheels of the pioneer wagons, the railroad and progress.

ADDENDUM 1

SHORTER COUNTY, NEBRASKA TERRITORY
1860 Nebraska Territorial Census and Mortality Schedule

Shorter County, Nebraska Territory
1860 Nebraska Territorial Census

No exact locations are shown for this census, except the post office is consistently shown on all four pages as being O'Fallons Bluff. The enumerator visited his subjects from west to east. The name shown on the Assistant Marshall line of the census was Sterrit M. Currant.

There were 114 people enumerated, 15 of whom were adults who could not read or write. Twenty three were born in a foreign country. There were eight unoccupied dwellings. The oldest person living in the county was Joseph Jewett, age 88 and the youngest was the 4 month old son of Charles and Orra McDonald. There were 16 traders, with John (Jack) Morrow, William S. Comstock and Joseph Jewett, listed specifically as Indian traders.

8 June 1860

1-1   Crawford Moore, 24 or 29, Trader, 3,000-2,050, b. New York
      Benjammin Grimes, 22, Clerk, 2000-300, b. Missouri
      Store and dwelling

3-2   Samuel Howe, 34, Carpenter, ----300, b. New Hampshire
      Sarah F., 24 or 26, b. Massachusetts
      Susan E., 3, b. New Hampshire

4-   F.C. Stewart, 24, Laborer, b. Ohio (can't read or write)
      Antoine Bergher, 24, Teamster, b. Canada
          (can't read or write)

5-3   Thomas Conroy, 31, Blacksmith, ----300, b. Ireland
      A. Saunderberg, 26, Blacksmith, b. Belgium

6-4   Robert Williams, 38, Trader, ----1,500, b. Ireland
      Fanny, 30, b. Missouri
      Christian, 8, b. Nebraska (male)
      Anna, 4, b. Nebraska
      Isabella, 3, b. Nebraska
      George, 7/12, b. Nebraska
      James A. Shiland, 23, Clerk, ----100, b. New York

7-5   F.M. Scott, 29, Blacksmith, ----200, b. Canada
       James P. Alber, 22, Blacksmith, ----150, b. Pennsylvania

8-   Unoccupied

9-6   David Christopher, 28, Stone Mason, ----100, b.Pennsylvania
       Nancy, 27, b. Ohio
       Columbus, 3, b. Iowa

June 9, 1860

10-7   R.W. White, 25, Stage Agent, ----500, b. New York

11-   P.P. Express and California Stage Co. Station
12-   Eating and Boarding House
13-   Sleeping and Ware House
14-   Daniel Chamberlain, 23, Station Keeper, b. Vermont
       John Carr, 24, Stage Driver, b. Illinois
       William Leach, 25, Stage Driver, b. Illinois
       James Stewart, 22, Stage Driver, b. Pennsylvania
       George McKenna, 23, Carpenter, ----500, b. Pennsylvania
       James Kneen, 26, Carpenter, ----200, b. Isle of Man

15-8   William Bishop, 25, Trader, ----500, b. Bavaria
       A.C. Shaw, 17, Clerk, b. Michigan

page 2
16-9   John A. Morrow, 28, Indian Trader, ----10,000 b. Pensylvania
       John Robinson, 26, clerk, 1,000----, b. Maryland
       Thomas Wilson, 23, Laborer, b. Maryland

17-10 Hugh Morgan, 25, Trader, ----10,000, b. Pennsylvania
       Edward Lane, 22, Clerk, ----100, b. Pennsylvania
       David Peck, 31, Laborer, b. Virginia

18-11 Charles Burke, 25, Landlord, ----500, b. Virginia
       George Gordon, 22, Teamster, b. Ireland
              (can't read or write)
       Franklin Lutz, 23, Teamster, b. Michigan

19-   Unoccupied

20-12 Joseph Jewett, 88, Indian Trader, 15,000-500
       b. France (can't read or write)
       Sarah, 25, (Indian), b. Nebraska
       Baptise, 10, b. Nebraska
       O.H. Olmstead, 23, Carpenter, ---500, b. New York
       Wilson Fleming, 19, Trapper, b. Mississippi
       (can't read or write)
       Thomas O'Flanigan, 28, Ditcher, b. Ireland

June 12, 1860

21-13 William S. Comstock, 21, Indian Trader, ----500,
       b. Wisconsin
       Constant Prenat, 35, (male), Laborer, ----100,
       b. France
       Thomas Lin, 27, Laborer, b. Vermont

22-   Unoccupied

June 13, 1860

23-14 Charles Hinman, 25, Trader, ----3,000, b. Pennsylvania
       Clara, 25 (Indian), b. Nebraska
       (can't read or write)
       Thomas Hays, 21, Clerk, b. Ohio
       James Bailey, 38, Laborer, b. Indiana

24-15 Joseph Croteau, 55, Trader, ---250, b. Canada
       (can't read or write)
       Angelina, 36, b. Missouri
       (can't read or write)
       Joseph, 12, b. Missouri
       John, 3, b. Missouri

25-   Leon Dufame, 17, Clerk, b. Missouri

26-   P.P. Express and California Stage Co. Station ----5,000
       John S. North, 26, Station Keeper, ----200, b. New York
       John Vill, 30, Laborer, ---100 b. Alabama
       James Leacock, 40, Carpenter, 6,000-45, b. Ireland
       Thomas Conrad, 25, Carpenter, b. Ireland
       William Rudd, 19, Herdsman, b. England
       Thomas Day, 22, Herdsman, b. New York

page 3
27-   Henry Gist, 28?, Carpenter, ----150, b. New York
      Franklin Tower, 24, Stagedriver, b. Louisiana
      Arthur Stephensen, 23, Stagedriver, b. Louisiana
      Henry Barber, 18, Laborer, b. Wisconsin

28-   Henry Bartlett, 21, Laborer, b. Illinois
      William Hall, 21, Laborer, b. Kentucky
      William Bartley, 22, Laborer, b. Kentucky
29-   Kitchen and Sleeping Rooms
30-   Dwelling and Ware House
31-   Unoccupied
32-   Sleeping Rooms for Passengers

33-17 Charles McDonald, 32, Trader, ----1,000, b. Tennessee
      Orra B., 20, b. New York
      James, 4/12, b. Nebraska
      George Miller, 24, Clerk, b. Pennsylvania

June 14, 1860

34-18 Isadore Boyer, 30, Trader, ----800, b. Missouri
      Samuel Key, 22, Clerk, b. Indiana

35-   George Porter, 32, Blacksmith, ----300, b. New York

36-   Unoccupied

37-18 William Roatch, 30, Baker, ----150, b. New York
          (can't read or write)

38-20 Camille Peck or Pelk, 22, Trader, ----300, b. Canada
      Theophilus LaConde, 25, Laborer, b. Canada
          (can't read or write)
      Robert North, 30, Laborer, ----50, b. Louisiana
      John Spanard, 28, Laborer, b. Mexico
          (can't read or write)
      Antoine, 22, Laborer, b. Mexico
          (can't read or write)
          (no surname given)

39-21 Joseph Gassman, 57, Physician, ----150, Prussia

40-22 William Fox, 29, Trader, ----500, b. New York
       Thomas Hoskins, 47, Laborer, ----100, b. New York

41-   Unoccupied

June 15, 1860

42-23 Z.B. Linder, 33, Farmer, ----1,000, b. Ohio
       Charles Green, 23, Farmer, ----50, b. Ireland

43-24 Samuel Machett, 30, Trader, ----5,000, b. Missouri
       Susan, 17, b. Missouri
       Lucy Riley, 30, Cook, b. Ireland
       William H. Sexton, 24, Clerk, b. Missouri

page 4
44-25 P.W. Chick, 24, Clerk, 1,000-200, b. Missouri
       Mary C. Chick, 20, b. Missouri

45-26 Peter C. Harvey, 34, Laborer, 1,000-600, b. Pennsylvania
       Mary, 28, (Indian), b. Nebraska
           (can't read or write)
       Mary, 8, b. Nebraska
       Charles, 5, b. Nebraska
       Juliana, 4, b. Nebraska
       John, 3, b. Nebraska

46-27 Charles Peterson, 28, Teamster, b. Hanover
           (can't read or write)
       Robert Lewis, 24, Teamster, b. Missouri
       Henry Bradley 26, Carpenter, ----500, b. Missouri

47-28 George W. Clark, 27, Trader, ----400, b. Vermont
       Charles M. Sexton, 22, Clerk, b. New York
       John Zeeps, 45, Laborer, b. Bohemia
           (can't read or write)

48-29 John Gilman, 25, Trader, ----1,500, b. New Hampshire
       H.C. Clifford, 25, Laborer, b. Indiana

49-30 John H. Dauchy, 25, Hotel keeper, ---1,000, b. New York
       J.K. Gillman, 28, Clerk, ----800, b. New Hampshire

50- Unoccupied

28 June 1860

51   P.P. Express and California Stage Co. Station ----3,000
52-31 Franklin Monroe, 35, Station Keeper, ---200, b. Pennsylvania
       Elmira, 19, House Keeper, b. Pennsylvania
       Henry Dillon, 23, Herdsman, b. Massachusetts
       Alfred Frink, 35, Stagedriver, b. Ohio

53- Unoccupied

MORTALITY SCHEDULE
SHORTER COUNTY, NEBRASKA
1860 Nebraska Territorial Census

Schedule 3; Deaths from 1860 Federal Census of Nebraska Territory, for the 12 months prior to 30 June 1860.

Nelson Boyer, 35, male, b. Missouri, no month of death shown, trader, died of convulsions in Shorter County.

A.S. Dow, 50, married or widowed, b. New Hampshire, d. June, emigrant struck by lightning, ill 1 day, died in Shorter County.

Henry Evans, 40, married or widowed, b. Indiana, d. October, emigrant died of exposure, ill 3 days, died in Shorter County.

Thomas Rice, 35, married or widowed, b. Michigan, d. April, emigrant, accidentally shot, ill 2 days, died in Shorter County.

John Taylor, 35, b. Ohio, d. November, stage driver, bleeding of lungs, ill 15 days, died in Shorter County.

Triefie, ---, age 23, male b. Kaw River, Kansas, died July, trader, died of snake bite, ill 3 days, died in Shorter County.

ADDENDUM 2

Pre-Statehood
Marriages
of
Shorter/Lincoln County,
Nebraska Territory

PRE-STATEHOOD MARRIAGES OF SHORTER/LINCOLN COUNTY, NEBRASKA TERRITORY

The following marriage abstracts were made from the original marriage records which are in the Nebraska State Historical Society, Lincoln, Nebraska. Copies of most of these also exist in bound volumes in the Lincoln County Courthouse, Office of County Judge, North Platte, Nebraska.

The format used for abstracting these records consists of Date of Marriage; Place of Marriage; Official, i.e. judge or minister; Groom; Groom's age; Groom's place of residence; Groom's place of birth; Bride's name; Bride's age; Bride's place of residence; Bride's place of birth; parents; witnesses; additional remarks. The spellings are shown as found on the documents. Some may differ from one document to the next as most of the clerks, government officials or ministers had some difficulty with spelling, particularly the names of German and Swedish individuals.

Most of the early marriages were performed by a judge or justice of the peace. The first marriage was performed in January of 1861 by Charles McDonald who came to Shorter County in 1860 and resided at Cottonwood Springs.

1861

10 January 1861 at Cottonwood Springs by Charles McDonald, Probate Judge
Camile Pettier, 21, res Cottonwood Springs
Melinda Hall, 21, res Cottonwood Springs
Wit: John Hanslip and George W. Clark
First marriage in Lincoln County (Shorter County)

1862

31 January 1862 at Cottonwood Springs by Charles McDonald, Judge
Harvey S. Merriman, 21, res Cottonwood Springs
Jane Casey, 21, res Cottonwood Springs

12 July 1862 by Chas. McDonald, Judge
Thomas M. Ballard, res Midway; b. Iowa
Martha Shafer, res. Midway; b. Iowa
Wit: D.L. Smith

1863

28 Sept. 1863 by G.A. Adams, Chaplin, 11th O V C
Major Boliver C. Converse of 11th Ohio Cav.
Mrs. Mary P. Parrish, of Cincinnati

21 May 1863 at Cottonwood Springs by Chas. McDonald, Judge
Robert Rowland, 21, res Cottonwood Springs
Dolly Grooms, 18, res Cottonwood Springs

27 Aug. 1863 at Cottonwood Springs by Chas. McDonald, Judge
Friend Dickenson, 21, res Cottonwood Springs
Sara Julite Luddington, 21, res Cottonwood Springs

14 Sept. 1863 at Cottonwood Springs by Chas. McDonald, Judge
Washington M. Hinman, 21, res Cottonwood Springs
Virginia Hill, 21, res Cottonwood Springs
Wit: H.C. Wright
[Note: Washington Mallory Hinman passed through what was to become Lincoln County in 1849 on his way to California. He returned from California in about 1854 and a few years later settled at Cottonwood Springs, establishing a ranch four miles from the spring. He served as an Indian interpreter from 1864-1867 at Fort McPherson. He was county treasurer of Shorter County in 1860 and later for Lincoln County.]

1864

4 June 1864 at Cottonwood Springs by Chas. McDonald, Judge
Edward Durkin of Cottonwood
Martha Sutton of Cottonwood

1865

12 Jan. 1865 at Cottonwood Springs by Chas. McDonald, Judge
Samuel D. Fitchie, 21 res Cottonwood
Ruhamah Helen Baker, 18, res Cottonwood

6 June 1865 at Cottonwood Springs by Chas. McDonald, Judge
Thomas Lewis, 21, res Cottonwood
Deby (Debby) Ann Lowe, 21, res Cottonwood

1866

19 Nov. 1866 by S.D. Fitchie, Judge
George Shaw
Miss Rebecah Swartz

7 March 1866 at Fort Heath by Charles McDonald, Probate Judge
Theodore I. Parker, 21, res Cottonwood Springs
Lucinda A. Rogers, 21, res Cottonwood Springs
[Note: Fort Heath was a military encampment west of North Platte, near present day Sutherland. Some military personnel are shown at Fort Heath on the 1870 Federal Census.]

15 May 1866 at Cottonwood Springs by Charles McDonald, Probate Judge
Henry P. Lawson, 21, res Cottonwood Springs
Charllotta Randell, 21, res Cottonwood Springs

10 May 1866 at Cottonwood Springs by S.D. Fitchie, Probate Judge
James A. Lee, 21, res Cottonwood Springs
Angeline C. Whitehead, 21, res Cottonwood Springs

9 November 1866 at Cottonwood by S.D. Fitchie
George Shaw, 21, res North Platte
Rebecka Swartz, 21, res North Platte

7 Dec. 1866
James A. Fagan
Miss Josephine Huff
A.L. Brown, signed application

9 December 1866 in Lincoln County by Frank Matter, Sixth Missionary
James Fagan, lawful age, res Lincoln County
Josephine Huff, lawful age, res Lincoln County
Wit: P.B. Enos and Charles Kennady of Cotton Springs (sic)
[Note: the above record was most likely the license taken out 7 December 1866 and 9 Dec 1866 was the marriage date.]

ADDENDUM 3

Commanding Officers
of
Fort Cottonwood/Fort McPherson

The following is a chronological list of the officers who served as Commanding Officers at Fort Cottonwood/Fort McPherson from 1863 to statehood in 1867.

Major George M. O'Brien - 7th Iowa Vol. Cav.
    first to serve as commander
    from September 27, 1863 until Sept. 28, 1864

Colonel S.W. Summers - 7th Iowa Vol. Cav.
    from September 28, 1864 until January 14, 1865

Captain Charles F. Porter - 1st Nebraska Veteran Cav.
    from January 14, 1865 until February 11, 1865

Major George M. O'Brien - 7th Iowa Vol. Cav.
    from February 11, 1865 until August 4, 1865

Lieutenant-Colonel William Baumer - 1st Nebr. Vet. Cav.
    from August 4, 1865 until September 16, 1865

Major Thomas J. Majors - 1st Nebr. Vet. Cav.
    from September 16, 1865 until December 24, 1865

Lieutenant-Colonel R.E. Fleming - 6th West Virginia
    Veteran Volunteer Cavalry
    from December 24, 1865 until April 5, 1866

Major Henry Norton - 6th U.S. Vol. Infantry
    from April 5, 1866 until about July 14, 1866

Captain Bvt. Lieutenant-Colonel J.K. Mizner - Second U.S.
    Cavalry
    from about July 14, 1866 until March 4, 1867

ADDENDUM 4

County Commissioner Records
Lincoln County, Nebraska
October, 1866

The following extracted information is from the first bound volume of County Commissioner Records in the County Clerk's office, Lincoln County Courthouse, North Platte, Nebraska. This is the only information pertaining to county commissioner meetings held in 1866 and the only records prior to Nebraska statehood March 1, 1867.

Territory of Nebraska
Lincoln County

At a meeting of the Board of County Commissioners within and for said County on Monday the first day of October AD 1866 there being present and acting W.M. Hinman and J.C. Gilman Commissioners at Cottonwood Springs being the first meeting of Commissioners Court after the organization of said Lincoln County in said Territory of Nebraska, the following business was transacted.

It was ordered by the said Board that said Lincoln County be divided into three Commissioners districts as follows to wit:
All that portion of Lincoln County lying east of Moran canon, commonly known as four mile canon, and west of a certain Ravine known and described as Snake ravine which crosses the main road immediately east of Wright and Jeffries ranch shall be known and designated as District No. one. All the portion of said county lying east of said Snake ravine and the eastern boundary of said Lincoln County shall be known and designated as District No. two And all that portion of said county lying west of said Moran or four mile canion and east of the Western boundary of said County shall be known and designated as District No. three.

On motion Board adjourned to meet at Cottonwood Springs in said County on Tuesday the 2nd day of October 1866.
    Chas McDonald
    County Clerk

The Board of County Commissioners met pursuant to adjournment at Cottonwood Springs Lincoln County Nebraska Territory at 10 o'clock AM Tuesday October 2nd 1866. Present W.M. Hinman, J.C. Gilman and J.A. Morrow, Commissioners.

It was ordered by the Board that an Election be held at the

house of Chas. McDonald in Cottonwood Springs Precinct of Lincoln County, Nebraska Territory on Tuesday the 9th day of October 1866 for the following offices. one delegate to Congress one Territorial Auditor one Territorial Treasurer one Territorial Librarian one Councilman and one Representative to the Territorial Legislature one Senator and one Representative to the State Legislature one Member to the 40th Congress of the United States one County Commissioner for the 2nd District one Coroner one Prosecuting Attorney Three Judges and two Clerks of Election, and that the proper notice be given accordingly.

Ordered by the Board the County Clerk be authorised to procure suitable Books for the use of the county and also a Seal for the use of the Office of the County Clerk.

The Official Bonds of Wm Baker Sheriff S.D. Fitchie Probate Judge and I.P. Boyer were approved and filed by the Board. On motion the Board adjourned to meet at the same place on Monday at 10 oclock a.m. October 8th 1866.

    Chas McDonald
    County Clerk

The Board of County Commissioners met pursuant to adjournment at Cottonwood Springs Lincoln County Nebraska Territory, at 10 o'clock a.m. October 8th 1866. Present W.M. Hinman, J.A. Morrow and J.C. Gilman, County Commissioners of said Lincoln County.

Ordered by the Board that all that portion of Lincoln County lying west of a line running north and south one mile east of old Fort Heath and the western boundary of said territory, be designated and established as Alkali Precinct and that elections shall be held therein at the House of E.B. Murphy in said precinct.

On motion the Court adjourned until court in course.

    Chas McDonald
    County Clerk

ADDENDUM 5

Peniston & Miller
Account Ledger
January 1, 1867 - February 29, 1867

In the 10 year span of time from the 1860 Nebraska Territorial Census when the area was known as Shorter County until the 1870 Federal Census when it was Lincoln County, there were many people coming and going through the county boundaries. Because of the time period, the nature of their lives and the lack of records, it is difficult to determine who was actually there.

Through the Account Ledger book of the store kept by Peniston and Miller in North Platte, we are able to piece together names and dates just prior to statehood. The entries begin with January 1, 1867 and for the two month period include the following.

January 1, 1867
General Casement
Capt. Clayton
A.T. Bird
Chas. Weed
McManus
Peter Manning
O.M. Fisher
S.E. Angle
Thomas Murry
Baker and Woodfull
John Richmond
Capt. Reed
Mr. Leighton
Hobbs
Jack A. Morrow
George Keck
Hiram Whitmarsh
Mr. Burk
John Burk
H. M. Carter
J.D. Sutherland
McDarmont
James Bates
Charles Seymore
James McClallen
W. Woodward
George Clark
Thomas O. Grad
Hiram Cressman

Henry Borgmeier
Thomas Turnbolt
W.H. Welty
George Soomis
Brady and Mores
January 6, 1867
    Wells Fargo and Co.
    James K. Ish
    M. Hellman
    Milton and Rodgers
    O.P. Ingalls and Co.
    Willis and Anderson
    John M. Connell and Co.
    Pollard and Patrick
    Thomas Murray
    M.S. and J.H. Reynolds
    John M. McCormick
    C.W. Burt
    G.R. Smitt
    Jordan and Graff
    McGath and Bros. and Co.
    Ketchum and Burns
    J.K. Ish and Co.
January 12, 1867
    M. Hellman and Co.
    James K. Ish
    Barklow and Bros Co.
    John M. Cormic and Co.
    Ketchum and Burns
    Midway Ranch
    McGath Bros. and Co.
    Milton Rodgers
    Welch
    George Glines
January 13, 1867
    Henry Borgmeier
    Jordan and Graffs
    S.E. Angle
    Wells Fargo and Co.
    John Wolfull
    Walter Touse
    F. Dickason
January 14, 1867

Henry Midcaff
F. Dickason
Thomas Willis
Stewart and Stevens
January 15, 1867
  H.M. Canter
  Capt. Reed
  Peter Manning
  Mack Donald
  Bird
  Leighton
January 16, 1867
  O.M. Fisher
  W.H. Welty
  Dick McMurry
  Thomas Turnbolt
  John Burk
  Mabin
January 17, 1867
  Mabin
  Brady andMoore
  John Burk
  F. Dickinson
  T.A. Turnbolt
  F. Dickason
  Genl. Casement
January 18, 1867
  Henry Borgmier
  Z. Stevens
  Joseph Chartrand
  Hiram Whitmarsh
  George R. Smith
  Poland and Patrick
January 24, 1867
  Hiram Whitmarsh
  O.M. Fisher
  Burk
  Henry Midcaff
  Hyatt and Henshaw
  J. K. Ish
  M.S. and J.K. Reynolds
  Henry Bird
  Capt. Reed

Jack Jones
January 25, 1867
    Capt. Clayton
    F. Dickason
    W.M. Hinman
    S.D. Fitchie
    Boies and Burk
    Thomas Turnbolt
    Henry Borgmier
    General Casement
    Henry Midcalf
    Wm. Touse
    Peter Manning
    W.H. Wetey
    Stephens Strickley
January 26, 1867
    Thomas A. Turnbolt
    Wm. Touse
    Whitmarsh & Co.
    Henry Bergmeier
    John Woodfull
    Brady and Moore
    J. Frichardson
January 27, 1867
    H. Whitmarsh
    Geo. Glines
    Henry Bergmeier
    Whitmarsh & Co.
    George Keck
    A. Miller
    Thomas McCarthy
    A.J. Armstrong
    Capt. Reed
    Jack Jones
    Walter Touse
    Wm. Hinman
    Chas. Powers
    W. Peniston
January 28, 1867
    Parks and Burt
    Henry Bergmeier
    Walter Touse
    George Glines

Geo. Turner & Co.
Midcaffs
January 31, 1867
Jack Jones
Leighton
Georg Glines
Whitmarsh and Co.
W.H. Welty
Thomas Turnbolt
February 1, 1867
Henry Bergmier
Thomas A. Turnbolt
A. Bird
Brady and Moore
Brice and Birk
Leighton
Henry Medcalf
T. Dickason
Jack Jones
MacDonald
Geo. Oaks
Gen. Casement
Wells Fargo & Co.
Peter Manning
Z. Stephens
W.H. Welty
February 2, 1867
Bayaye Master
Henry Metcalfe
Capt. Reed
Walter Touse
Henry Bergmier
Leighton
Thos. A. Turnbull
O.M. Fisher
J. Burt
Stewart & Stephens
John Burk
Jack Jones
February 4, 1867
Peter Manning
F. Dickason
Julius Coffe

Thos. Willis
Gen. Casement
February 6, 1867
    Midway
    Henry Borgmeier
    A.J. Miller
    O.P. Ingalds & Co.
    Wm. S. Peniston
    Milton and Rodgers
    Megath & Co.
    D. Whitney & Co.
    F. Dickasons
February 7, 1867
    O.M. Fisher
    Willis and Anderson
    Henry Bergmeier
    Leighton
    Hinman & Co.
    Misso (?) Clary & Co.
    Tim Slaptiton
    Thomas Reynolds
    Arthur McClary
    Jim Brannan
    Pat Brenan
    Tim Brannan
February 9, 1867
    O.M. Fisher
    F.N. Turnbull
    F. Dickason
    Stewart & Stephens
February 10, 1867
    Henry Borgmeier
    John Wolfull
    McDonald
    T.A. Turnbull
    W.H. Welty
    T.A. Bird
    John Burk
    Z. Stewart & Stephens
    Leighton
    Capt. Reed
    Gen. Casement
    Walter Touse

John Richmond
Henry Metcalfe
O.M. Fisher
H. Pether
T. Dickinson
Jack Jones
Peter Manning
February 12, 1867
Jack Jones
S.E. Leighton
John Richmond
Stewart and Stephen
Peter Maning
Pether
T.A. Turnboll
W.H. Weley
Capt. W. Woodward
Charley M. Cook
Major O'Brien
Thomas A. Turnbull
McDonald
Henry Metcalfe
February 15, 1867
F. Dickason
Stewart & Stephens
Walter Touse
Gen. Casement
Leighton
Henry Brgmiser
February 20, 1867
Jordan and Graff
Henry Pether
Wells Fargo & Co.
Walter Touse
Henry Metcalfe
Henry Brgmeier
S.E. Layton
Peter Maning
George Glines
Chas. Powers
T.A. Turnbolt
Gen. Casement
Stewart & Stephen

Brice & Burk
Capn. Reed
F. Dickinson
J. Richmond
Mr. Hall
John Burk
Thomas More
February 21, 1867
    Henry Bergmeier
    Z. Stewart & Stephens
    George R. Smith
    John Burk
    Cap. Reed
February 23, 1867
    John Weolfull
    H. Pether
    Henry Bergmire
    Wigeatt Bros. & Co.
    Whitmarsh & Co.
February 24, 1867
    Whitmarsh
    A. Miller
    T.A. Miller
    A.T. Bird
    D.L. Trout
    O.M. Fisher
February 25, 1867
    John Bowen
    Stewart & Stephens
    Walter Touse
    F. Dickinson
    Thomas A. Turnbull
    Layton
February 26, 1867
    Jack Jones
    Geo. Glines
    Gen. Casement
    J. Burt
    Stewart & Stephens
    Henry Bergmier
    F. Dickinson
    Wells Fargo & Co.
    H. Metcalfe

Layton
February 28, 1867
John Burkhard
John Wolfull
Thom. A. Turnbull
Cap. Reed
Henry Pether
Jack Jones
Stewart & Stephens
Walter Touse
February 29, 1867
Walter Touse
Jas. Powers
Henry Pether
A.J. Bird
Peter Manning
Dan Trout
Whitmarsh & Co.
O.M. Fisher
Thos. Turnbull
Stewart & Stephens
Jack Jones
F. Dickinson
Layton
Geo. Glines
Henry Bergmeier
Henry Metcalfe
M. Hellman
Melton Rodgers
Poland & Patrick
J.M. Cormilk
C.W. Burt
J.M. Cormicks
C.W. Burts

The spellings of names was not consistent throughout these records. In some cases the surname only was used. The merchandise prices are interesting to note:

cans of oysters at $1.75; pork at 20 cents per pound; corn at 4 1/2 cents per pound; coffee at 45 cents per pound; nails at 15 cents per pound; pants at $5; plug of tobacco 40 cents; pairs of socks 60 cents; lineament 50 cents a bottle; undershirts at $3.00; overshirts at

$5.50; muscat wine $2.00 a bottle; cigars $1.00; mittens $1.00 pair; cocane $1.00; knives $2.00 each; combs 45 cents each; syrup $3.00 gallon; candles 40 cents a pound; soap 25 cents; tooth brushes 75 cents; cinamond (sic) $1.00 pound; lard at 35 cents per pound; brooms 40 cents; tea at $2.00 per pound; vinegar $1.20 a gallon; whiskey $4.00 a gallon; playing cards 50 cents a deck; woolen blankets $9.00 each.

One of the most expensive items was a buffalo robe sold to Bayaye Master on account, February 2, 1867 for $14.00. Peniston and Miller dealt in everything needed for life on the frontier. According to entries in their account book they provided people also with breakfast and supper and borrowed and loaned money. On February 19, 1867 they loaned $250.00 by express to First National Bank in Omaha. The express charge was figured in at $1.50.

From their store in North Platte, Penniston and Miller traded as far east as Willow Island and Brady Island.

ADDENDUM 6

Pre-Statehood Towns and Villages of Lincoln County, Nebraska

The following are pre-statehood towns and villages of Lincoln County, Nebraska.

CAMP SERGEANT - A small military outpost at North Platte, established during the construction of the Union Pacific Railroad to protect rail line workers from the Indians.

COLD SPRINGS - Nebraska Pony Express Station No. 22; located on Box Elder Creek south and west of North Platte.

COTTONWOOD - Post office established April 17, 1860; name changed to Cottonwood Falls on October 19, 1860. Named for cottonwood trees in the area.

COTTONWOOD FALLS - Post office named changed from Cottonwood on October 19, 1860; named changed to Cottonwood Springs on January 8, 1861.

COTTONWOOD SPRINGS - Post office name changed from Cottonwood Falls on January 8, 1861; discontinued April 11, 1895. First county records were kept here. Served as a county seat until the Union Pacific Railroad and the town of North Platte were established. Records were transferred to North Platte on November 12, 1867.

DANSEY'S - Nebraska Pony Express Station No. 24; located south and west of the present town of Sutherland. Sometimes called Elkhorn or Halfway House.

FORT COTTONWOOD - Originally named Fort McKean in 1863, this military post became Fort Cottonwood in May of 1864. Two years later it was changed to Fort McPherson.

FORT McKEAN - Military post established in 1863 and named in honor of Major Thomas J. McKean, commanding officer of the western territory of the Platte Valley. Sometimes called Cantonment McKean.

FORT McPHERSON - Named in 1866 in honor of Major General James B. McPherson, killed in the Civil War. Cavalry stationed here played an important role in guarding the immigrants and protecting cattle ranches. The fort was in continuous use until 1880, when it was abandoned. A National Cemetery was established near there in 1873.

FORT HEATH - A military outpost located near O'Fallons Bluff;

established by 1866. Named either for General H.H. Heath of the 7th Iowa Cavalry or his son, Lt. George W. Heath, who was killed at Cottonwood Springs in 1864.

FREMONT SPRINGS - Nebraska Pony Express Station No. 23; located near the present town of Hershey. Sometimes referred to as Buffalo Ranch. Named for General John C. Fremont.

GILMANS - Nebraska Pony Express Station No. 19; located in southwest Lincoln County. The owners were John and Jeremiah Gilman, natives of New Hampshire.

MACHETTE'S - Nebraska Pony Express Station No. 20; located on the William's Upper 96 Ranch, east of Fort McPherson.

MIDWAY - Post office established May 19, 1865; discontinued February 13, 1867; probably named for its central location in the county.

NORTH PLATTE - Post office established February 13, 1867. County seat was laid out for the Union Pacific Railroad by General G.M. Dodge in 1866. Situated on the North Platte River; county seat of Lincoln County.

O'FALLONS - Post office established in 1883; changed to Hershey in 1890. This junction point on the railroad received its name from a nearby bluff, probably named for Major Benjamin O'Fallon, soldier, Indian agent and trader.

PAWNEE - Post office established March 24, 1854; discontinued July 1, 1857. The site later became a station on the Union Pacific Railroad known as Pawnee; named for the Indian tribe.

BIBLIOGRAPHY

BIBLIOGRAPHY

Adamson, Archibald R. *North Platte and Its Associations.* The Evening Telegraph, North Platte, 1910.

Ames, Charles Edgar. *Pioneering the Union Pacific, A Reappraisal of the Builders of the Railroad.* Appleton-Century-Crofts, New York, 1969.

Andreas, A.T. *History of the State of Nebraska.* The Western Historical Company, Chicago, 1882.

Athearn, Robert G. *Union Pacific Country.* Rand McNally & Company, 1971.

Bare, Ira L. and Will H. McDonald, eds. *An Illustrated History of Lincoln County, Nebraska and Her People.* 2. volumes. The American Historical Society, 1920.

Bratt, John. *Trails of Yesterday.* University Publishing Co., Lincoln, 1921.

Bruff, J. Goldsborough. *Gold Rush: [His] Journals, Drawings, and Other Papers.* ed. Georgia Willis Read and Ruth Gaines. New York, 1944.

Carpenter, Allan. *The New Enchantment of Nebraska.* Childrens Press, Chicago, 1978.

Coleman, Ruby. "Colorful Characters Like Leon Pallardy Helped Shape Plains History," *Heritage Lines; North Platte Telegraph*, January 25, 1989.

-----------. "Courage Was Common Denominator," *Heritage Lines; North Platte Telegraph*, May 25, 1988.

-----------. "Journal Recounts Illness On the Westward Trail in 1849," *Heritage Lines; North Platte Telegraph*, October 17, 1990.

-----------. "Much-traveled Platte Valley Has Rich Heritage," *Heritage Lines; North Platte Telegraph*, February 7, 1990.

----------. "O'Fallon's Bluff Took a Day's Maneuvering," *Heritage Lines; North Platte Telegraph*, January 18, 1984.

----------. "Pioneers Faced, Conquered the Great American Desert," *Heritage Lines; North Platte Telegraph*, August 5, 1987.

----------. "Seeing 'The Elephant'," Heritage Lines; North Platte Telegraph, March 2, 1988.

----------. "Tall Tales of Junction Ranch," Heritage Lines; North Platte Telegraph, July 23, 1986.

----------. "Unknown Soldier Was Known to Someone," *Heritage Lines; North Platte Telegraph*, May 23, 1984.

----------. "Vast Stretch of Open Prairie Greeted Pioneers Near NP," *Heritage Lines; North Platte Telegraph*, June 17, 1987.

----------. "Willow Street's Viaduct Crosses Military Post Site," *Heritage Lines; North Platte Telegraph*, September 11, 1985.

----------. "Trapper, Trader Follows Trails to North Platte," *Heritage Lines; North Platte Telegraph*, January 21, 1987.

Doetsch, Raymond N. *Journey to the Green and Golden Lands.* Kennikat Press, Port Washington, New York, 1976.

Drury, Clifford M. *Marcus and Narcissa Whitman and the Opening of Old Oregon*. Volume 1, Pacific Northwest National Parks & Forests Association, 1986.

Eide, Ingvard Henry. *Oregon Trail*. Rand, McNally & Company, 1972.

Fitzpatrick, Lilian L. *Nebraska Place Names.* University of Nebraska Press, 1960.

Franzwa, Gregory M. *Maps of the Oregon Trail.* The Patrice Press, Gerald, Missouri, 1982.

------------------. *The Oregon Trail Revisited.* The Patrice Press, Gerald, Missouri, 1972.

Gardiner, Dorothy. *West of the River.* Thomas Y. Crowell Co., 1941.

Grinnell, G.B. *The Fighting Cheyennes.* University of Oklahoma Press, 1956.

Groff, Jane, coordinator. *Nebraska Our Towns ... South Central.* Taylor Publishing Company, Dallas, Texas, 1988.

Hafen, LeRoy R. and Ann W. Hafen. *Handcarts to Zion.* The Arthur H. Clark Co., Glendale, California, 1960.

Hagerty, L.W. "Indian Raids Along the Platte and Little Blue Rivers," *Nebraska History*, XXVIII (July-September 1947), 176-86; (October-December, 1947), 239-60.

Hannon, Jessie Gould. *The Boston-Newton Company Venture from Massachusetts to California 1849.* Unviersity of Nebraska Press, 1969.

Holmes, Louis A. *Fort McPherson, Nebraska.* Johnsen Publishing Company, Lincoln, Nebraska, 1963.

Hutton, Mary S. *An Early History of North Platte, Nebraska.* Master's Thesis, University of Nebraska, Lincoln, July 1944.

Johnsgard, Paul A. *The Platte, Channels in Time.* University of Nebraska Press, 1984.

Lefdyard, Edgar M., ed. *A Journal of the Birmingham Emigrating Company by Leander V. Loomis.* Salt Lake City, Utah, 1928.

Mattes, Merrill J. *The Great Platte River Road.* University of Nebraska Press, 1969.

Meehan, Mary Jane. *The Saga of Brady Island.* Clark Hord Printing, North Platte, n.d.

Morton, J. Sterling. *Illustrated History of Nebraska.* Jacob North & Co., Lincoln, Nebraska, 1907.

Nimmo, Sylvia. *Maps Showing The County Boundaries of Nebraska, 1854-1925.* Papillion, Nebraska.

North Platte Genealogical Society. *A Research Guide to Genealogical Data In Lincoln County, Nebraska*. Nebraska State Genealogical Society, 1984.

Olson, James C. *History of Nebraska*. University of Nebraska Press, 1954; rev. ed., 1966.

Perkey, Elton A. *Perkey's Names of Nebraska Locations*.

Peterson, Nancy M. *People of the Moonshell, A Western River Journal*. Renaissance House, 1984.

Root, Frank A. and William Elsey Connelley. *The Overland Stage to California*. Topeka, Kansas, 1901.

Sheldon, Addison Erwin. *Nebraska The Land and The People*. Volume 1. The Lewis Publishing Co., 1931.

Vexler, Robert I. and William F. Swindler. *Chronology and Documentary Handbook of the State of Nebraska*. Oceana Publications, Inc. 1978.

Ware, Eugene F. *The Indian War of 1864*. University of Nebraska Press, 1960.

Weland, Gerald. *Last Post*. Heritage Books, Inc., 1989.

Yost, Nellie Snyder. *Buffalo Bill His Family, Friends, Fame, Failures and Fortunes*. Sage Books, The Swallow Press, Inc., Chicago, 1979.

--------------------. *The Call of the Range*. Sage Books, Denver, 1966.

Zabel, Harvey J. *History of Fort McPherson, Nebraska*. Master's Thesis, Colorado State College, Greeley, Colorado, 1954.

Brevet's Nebraska Historical Markers and Sites. Brevet Press, 1974.

Who's Who In Nebraska. Nebraska Press Association, Lincoln, 1940.

"Grave of Man Killed by Lightning Is Found," *North Platte Telegraph Bulletin*, July 17, 1963.

"Hinman Store Supplied Settlers, Fort," *North Platte Telegraph*, September 17, 1973.

"100 Years of Rolling by the River," *North Platte Telegraph*, September 17, 1973.

"Prophecy Warned of an Early-Day Tragedy," *North Platte Telegraph*, July 17, 1963.

"The Rails of Progress Are Laid; Moving Westward at Three Miles a Day," *North Platte Telegraph*, March 1, 1987.

"Rustic and Unimposing Though It May Have Been, John Burke's...," *North Platte Telegraph*, March 1, 1987.

"Stirring Tales of Cavalry and Indians Keep Alive Memory of Fort McPherson," *North Platte Telegraph*, March 1, 1987.

Account Ledger Book of Peniston and Miller Store, North Platte, Nebraska.

County Commissioner's Records; Lincoln County, Nebraska Courthouse.

1860 Nebraska Territorial Census; Shorter County.

Schedule 3; Deaths from 1860 Nebraska Territorial Census, Shorter County.

War of the Rebellion; Official Records of the Union and Confederate Armies; Series I. Vol. XXXIV, Parts I, II, III, IV, January 1, 1864 to June 30, 1864; Series I. Vol. XLI, Parts I, II, III, IV, July 1, 1864 to December 31, 1864; Series I. Vol. XLVIII, Parts I and II, January 1, 1865 to December 31, 1865.

INDEX

Adams, G.A.	100
Alber, James A.	92
Althimer & Co.	85
Amich, David	18
Anderson, Corporal	73
Andreas, A.T.	31, 34, 35
Angle, S.E.	113, 114
Antoine	94
Armstrong, A.J.	116
Ashley, William	10
Astor, John Jacob	9
Bad Wound	64, 65
Bailey, James	93
Baker and Woodful	113
Baker, Lou	37
Baker, Ruhamah Helen	100
Baker, William	28, 110
Ballard, Thomas	100
Barber, Henry	94
Barklow and Bros. Co.	114
Bartlett, Henry	94
Bartley, William	94
Bates, James	113
Baumer, Lt. Col. William	105
Beauvais, G.P.	55
Bergher, Antoine	91
Bergmeier, Henry	116, 188, 120, 121
Bergmier, Henry	117, 120
Bergmire, Henry	120
Big Mouth	42
Bird	115
Bird, A.	117
Bird, A.T.	113, 120
Bird, Henry	115
Bird, A.J.	121
Birge, Julius	78
Bishop, William	34, 92
Boies and Burk	116
Boon, Dr. J.T.	18
Booth, J. Wilkes	76
Bordeaux, James	55
Borgmeier, Henry	114, 118
Borgmier, Henry	115, 116

Boston Newton Company	20
Bourgmond, Etienne Veniard de	7
Bowen, John	120
Bower, Joe	35
Bowles, Samuel	30, 83
Boyer, Felix	35
Boyer, Isadore P.	27, 28, 94, 110
Boyer, Mr. and Mrs. Nelson	35
Boyer, Nelson	27, 96
Boyers	34
Bradley, Henry	95
Brady and Mores	114, 117
Brady and Moore	115, 116
Brannan, Jim	118
Brannan, Tim	118
Bratt, Elizabeth Burke	51
Bratt, John	44, 45, 50, 51
Brenan, Pat	118
Borgmeier, Henry	118
Brgmiser, Henry	119
Brice & Burk	117, 120
Bridger, Jim	10
Brown, A.L.	101
Bruff, Joseph Goldborough	18
Burk	115
Burk, John	113, 115, 117, 118, 120
Burk, Mr.	113
Burke, Charles	92
Burke, Daniel	48
Burke, Elizabeth "Lizzie"	51
Burke, Janie DeLong	24
Burke, John	48, 49, 50, 82, 86
Burke, Margaret	49
Burke, William	23
Burke-DeLong Wagon Train	23
Burkhard, John	121
Burt, C.W.	114, 121
Burt, Francis	27
Burt, J.	117, 120
Burts, C.W.	121
Canter, H.M.	115
Carr, John	92

Carter, H.M.	113
Carter, Levi	51
Casey, Jane	99
Chamberlain, Daniel	92
Charlot, Major C.S.	64, 65, 75
Chartrand, Joseph	115
Chase, Senator Salmon P.	81
Chick, Mary C.	95
Chick, P.W.	95
Chief Bad Wound	64
Chief Sleepy Eyes	83
Chief Two Ax	10
Chivington, Col. J.M.	63
Choteau, Auguste	8
Chateau, Pierre	8
Christopher, Columbus	92
Christopher, David	92
Christopher, Nancy	92
Clark, George	113
Clark, George W.	95, 99
Clark, William	9
Clary, Misso (?) & Co.	118
Clatyon, Capt.	113, 116
Clifford, H.C.	95
Clifford, Mortimer Harrison "Monty"	55
Clyman, James	10
Cody, William F.	29, 43, 55, 56
Coe, Isaac	51
Coffe, Julius	117
Collins, Colonel	63
Comstock, William S.	43, 91, 93
Con-qu-num-pa	65
Connell, John M. and Co.	114
Connor, Brig. Gen. P.E.	75, 76
Conrad, Thomas	93
Conroy, Thomas	91
Constant	43
Converse, Major Boliver C.	100
Cook, Charley M.	119
Corlew, John	46
Cormic, John M. and Co.	114
Cormicks, J.M.	121
Cormilk, J.M.	121

Coronado, Francisco Vasquez de	3
Creighton, Edward	31
Cremer, Lt. Harrison W.	72
Cressman, Hiram	113
Croteau, Angelina	93
Croteau, John	93
Croteau, Joseph	93
Cuming, Thomas B.	27
Cur-tig-a-lisha	65
Currant, Sterrit M.	91
Curtis, Major General	63, 69, 70, 71, 72
Darling, Dick	34
Dauchy, John H.	95
Davis, Mrs.	34
Day, Thomas	93
DeLong, Janie	23
DeLong, William	23
Dick, Dr. F.H.	85
Dickason, F.	115, 116, 118, 119
Dickason, T.	114, 117
Dickasons, F.	115, 118
Dickenson, Friend	100
Dickinson, F.	115, 120
Dickinson, T.	119
Dillon, Henry	96
Dodge, Col. Henry	11
Dodge, General Grenville M.	82, 87, 126
Dodge, Grenville M.	81
Dodge, Major-General G.M.	76
Doetsch, Raymond N.	17
Douglas, Senator Stephen A.	27
Dow, A.S.	96
Dow, Augustus S.	46
Dufame, Leon	93
Durant, Thomas	81
Durkin, Edward	100
Eagle Twice	64
Eaton, John	11
Enos, P.B.	86, 101
Ericsson, E.E.	41, 50
Evans, Governor	69
Evans, Henry	96
Evans, James W.	21

Everett, Edward	20
Fagan, James A.	101
Fillion, Joseph F.	56, 57
Fisher, O.M.	113, 115, 117, 118, 119, 120, 121
Fitchie, S.D.	28, 45, 46, 101, 110, 116
Fitchie, Sam	50
Fitchie, Samuel D.	100
Fitzpatrick, Lilian L.	47
Fitzpatrick, Thomas	10
Flanagan, Lt. Thomas	74
Fleming, Lt. Col. R.E.	105
Fleming, Wilson	93
Fox, William	95
Fremont, John C.	11, 126
Frichardson, J.	116
Frink, Alfred	96
Gallagher, Ben	48
Gallagher, Mary Ann	47
Gardipi	34
Gassman, Joseph	94
Gessner	83
Gillette brothers	69
Gilman, Edward	41
Gilman, Jeremiah	41, 126
Gilman, J.K.	95
Gilman, John	41, 126
Gillman, John	95
Gillman, J.C.	28, 109, 110
Gist, Henry	94
Glass, Hugh	10
Glines, Geo.	114, 116, 117, 119, 120, 121
Gordon, George	92
Gould, Charles	20
Grad, Thomas D.	113
Grant, Seth	10
Grattan, Lt.	55
Gray, Captain Pleasant	18
Green, Charles	95
Grimes, Benjamin	91
Grinnel, George B.	61

Grooms, Dolly	100
Gwin, Senator	29
Hall, Melinda	99
Hall, Mr.	120
Hance, Lt. Morgan A.	72
Hanslip, John	99
Harney	67
Harvey, Charles	95
Harvey, John	95
Harvey, Juliana	95
Harvey, Mary	95
Harvey, Peter C.	95
Hays, Thomas	93
Healy, William	86
Heath, Col.	76
Heath, General H.H.	32, 126
Heath, Lt. George W.	32, 126
Hellman, M.	114, 121
Hellman, M. and Co.	114
Henry, Orra B.	34
Hequembourg, C.L.	51
Hill, "Billy"	41
Hill, Virginia	42, 100
Hinman & Co.	118
Hinman, Beach Isaac	42, 86
Hinman, Charles	36, 42, 93
Hinman, Clara	93
Hinman, John F.	42
Hinman place	71
Hinman, Vaughan	42
Hinman, Washington Mallory	28, 41, 42, 56, 61, 68, 100, 109, 110, 116
Hobbs	113
Holladay, Ben	30, 48
Hoskins, Thomas	95
Howe, Samuel	91
Howe, Sarah F.	91
Howe, Susan E.	91
Huff, Miss Josephine	101
Hyatt and Henshaw	115
Ingalds, O.P. & Co.	118
Ingalls, O.P. and Co.	114

Ish, J.K.	114, 115
Ish, J.K. and Co.	114
Ish, James K.	114
Jackson, David E.	10
Janis, Antoine	55
Janis, Nicholas	55
Jefferson, President	9
Jewett, Baptise	93
Jewett, Joseph	91, 93
Jewett, Sarah	93
Jones, Jack	116, 117, 119, 120, 121
Jones, John S.	29
Jordan and Graff	114, 119
Jordan and Graffs	114
Keck, George	113, 116
Kennady, Charles	101
Ketchum and Burns	114
Key, Samuel	94
Kirby, Will	46
Kneen, James	92
Kuhl, Capt. Henry	72
l'Archeveque, Juan de	7
LaSalle	7
LaConde, Theophilus	94
Lane, Edward	92
Laughing Eyes	42
Lawson, Henry P.	101
Layton	120, 121
Layton, S.E.	119
Leach, William	92
Leacock, James	93
Leavenworth and Pikes Peak Express	29
Lee, James A.	101
Lee, Lemuel	18
Leighton	115, 117, 118, 119
Leighton, Mr.	113
Leighton, S.E.	119
Lester, Gurdon P.	32
Lewis, Capt. Meriwether	9
Lewis, Elias	22
Lewis, Robert	95
Lewis, Thomas	101

Lin, Thomas	93
Lincoln, President Abraham	28, 76
Linder, Z.B.	95
Little Thunder	65
Livingston, Colonel	72
Long Face	65
Long, Major Stephen H.	9
Loomis, Abner	19
Loomis, Adoniram Judson	19
Loomis, Andrew	19
Loomis, Leander Vaness	19
Lord, Brackett	20
Lord, Major	67
Lowe, Deby (Debby) Ann	101
Lower, Tom	47
Lucian, Augustine (Lucia)	55
Luddington, Sara Julie	100
Lutz, Franklin	92
Mabin	115
MacArthur, Capt. Arthur	78
MacArthur, General Douglas	78
Mac Donald	117
Mack Donald	115
Machett, Samuel	35, 95
Machett, Susan	95
Machette, J.	35
Majors, Major Thomas J.	105
Mallett, Paul	7
Mallett, Pierre	7
Maloy, Daniel	19
Maning, Peter	115, 119
Manning, Peter	113, 116, 117, 119, 121
Master, Bayaye	117, 122
Matter, Frank	101
Mattes, Merrill J.	35
McCarthy, Thomas	116
McClallen, James	113
McClanahan, J.M.	18
McClary, Arthur	118
McCormick, John M.	114
McCullough, John	47
McDarmont	113

McDonald	118, 119
McDonald, Charles	28, 34, 35, 42, 44, 86, 94, 99, 100, 101, 109, 110
McDonald, Frank	35
McDonald, James	94
McDonald, Mrs. Charles	71
McDonald, Orra B.	34, 94
McDonald, William H.	35
McGath and Bros. and Co.	114
McKean, Major Thomas J.	125
McKenna, George	92
McKenny, Major T.K.	65
McManus	113
McMurry, Dick	115
McPherson, Major Gen. James B.	78, 125
Medcalf, Henry	117
Megath & Co.	118
Meinhold, Capt. Charles	56
Merriman, Harvey S.	99
Metcalfe, H.	120
Medcalfe, Henry	117, 119, 120, 121
Midcaff, Henry	115
Midcalf, Henry	116
Midcaffs	116
Midway	118
Midway Ranch	114
Miller, A.	116, 120
Miller, A.J.	85, 118
Miller, George	94
Miller, T.A.	120
Milton and Rodgers	114, 118
Minguez, Father Juan	7
Mitchell, Capt.	73
Mitchell, General	63, 64, 65, 68, 69, 70, 71, 72, 74, 75
Mizner, Capt. Bvt. Lt. Col. J.K.	105
Monroe, Elmira	96
Monroe, Franklin	96
Moore, Crawford	37, 91
Moore, S.W.	18
More, Thomas	120
Morgan, Hugh	92

Morgan, Hugh "Hewey"	45
Morin, Edward de	55, 56, 57
Morin, Mrs. Valenteen	56
Morin, Valentine	56, 58
Morrow, John "Jack"	28, 36, 43, 45, 46, 51, 82, 91, 92, 109, 113
Morton, J. Sterling	49
Murphy, E.B.	110
Murray, Thomas	114
Murry, Thomas	113
Naranjo, Jose	7
North, John S.	36, 93
North, Justus S.	36
North, Major Frank	47
North, Robert	94
Norton, Major Henry	105
O'Brien, Capt.	68
O'Brien, Major G.M.	64, 65, 68, 70, 71, 76, 105, 119
O'Fallon, Major Benjamin	32, 126
O'Flanigan, Thomas	93
O'Sullivan, John L.	17
O-A-Sehu-Cha	65
Oaks, Geo.	117
Olmstead, O.H.	93
Pallardie, Eulalie Sarie	55
Pallardie, Francois Leon	55
Pallardie, Pierre	55
Pallerdy, Leon	55
Pallerdy, Valentine Morin	56
Palliday, Leon	55
Palmer, Joel	21
Parker, Theodore I.	32, 101
Parks and Burt	116
Parrish, Mrs. Mary P.	100
Parry, Major Henry C.	84
Patterson, E.H.N.	33
Patterson, John B.	77
Peater/Peters, Valentine	56
Peck, David	92
Peck/Pelk, Camille	94
Peniston and Miller	50, 85, 86, 122, 113

Peniston, W.	116
Peniston, William S.	85
Peniston, Wm. S.	118
Peters, Valentine	57
Peterson, Charles	95
Pether	119
Pether, H.	119, 120
Pether, Henry	119, 121
Pettier, Camille	99
Pierce, President	27
Poland & Patrick	115, 121
Pollard and Patrick	114
Porter, Capt. Charles F.	72, 105
Porter, George	94
Powers, Chas.	116, 119
Powers, Jas.	121
Pratt, Jno.	75
Pratt, John	68
Prenat, Constant	93
Prickley Pear	64
Randall, Tod	51
Randell, Charllotta	101
Rankin, Lt. John K.	71
Reed, Capt.	113, 115, 116, 117, 118, 120, 121
Reynolds, M.S. and J.H.	114
Reynolds, M.S. and J.K.	115
Reynolds, Thomas	118
Reynolds, William	72
Ribble, Capt. Henry H.	72
Rice, Thomas	96
Richmond, J.	120
Richmond, John	113, 119
Riley, Lucy	95
Roatch, William	94
Roberts, Ellenor	22
Robideaux, Joseph	27, 28
Robinson, John	92
Rodgers, Melton	121
Rodgers, Milton	114
Rogers, Lucinda	32, 101
Rose, Edward	10
Rowland, Bob	51

Rowland, Robert	100
Rudd, William	93
Russell, Majors and Waddell	29
Russell, William H.	29
Sanborn, General J.B.	56
Saunderberg, A.	91
Scott, F.M.	92
Seward, Secretary	76
Sexton, Charles M.	95
Sexton, William H.	95
Seymore, Charles	113
Shafer, Martha	100
Shantag-a-lisk	64
Sharp, Jack	51
Shaw, A.C.	92
Shaw, George	101
Sherman, General W.T.	56
Shiland, James A.	91
Simpson, General J.H.	83
Simpson, Lewis	29
Slaptiton, Tim	118
Smith, D.L.	100
Smith, Dan	76
Smith, George R.	115, 120
Smith, Jedediah	10
Smith, Lot	29
Smith-Jackson-Sublette	10
Smither, J.	118, 114
Smitt, G.R.	114
Snell, Jacob	41
Snyder, John	33
Soomis, George	114
Spalding, Elizabeth/Eliza	11
Spanard, John	94
Spalding, Rev. Henry Harmon	11
Spotted Tail	64, 65
Staples, David	20
Stephens, Z.	117
Stephensen, Arthur	94
Stevens, Z.	115
Stewart & Stephen	115, 117, 118, 119, 120, 121
Stewart, F.C.	91

Stewart, James	92
Stewart, Z. & Stephens	118, 120
Strickley, Stephens	116
Stuart, Robert	9
Summers, Colonel S.W.	71, 105
Sutherland, J.D.	113
Sutton, Martha	100
Swartz, Miss Rebecah	101
Swartz, Rebecka	101
Taylor, C.	18
Taylor, John	96
The Big Mandan	64
Touse, Walter	114, 116, 118, 119, 120, 121
Touse, Wm.	116, 117
Tower, Franklin	94
Triefie	96
Trout, D.L.	120
Trout, Dan	35, 121
Turgeon	51
Turnboll, T.A.	115, 119
Turnbull, F.N.	118
Turnbull, T.A.	118, 119
Turnbull, Thos. A.	117, 120, 121
Turnbolt, Thomas	116, 117
Turnbolt, Thomas A.	116, 119
Turner, Geo. and Co.	117
Two Crows	64, 65
Two Face	71
Two Strike	64, 65
Uhling, Otto	86
Vance, Tomas	19
Vasquez, Louis	10
Vaughan, Rebecca Franklin	42
Vilantry	34
Vill, John	93
Villasur, Don Pedro de	7
Wade, Rev. Benjamin	46, 47
Walen, Major H.D.	65
Ware, Eugene	33, 44, 62
Ware, Lt. Eugene F.	50
Waugh, Jno.	19
Webb, Anna	85

Weed, Chas.	113
Welch	114
Welch, Tom	83
Weley, W.H.	119
Wells Fargo & Co.	114, 117, 119, 120
Welty, W.H.	114, 117
Weolfull, John	120
Wetey, W.H.	115, 116
Whisler	65
White, R.A.	92
Whitehead, Angeline C.	101
Whitman, Marcus	12
Whitman, Narcissa	12
Whitman-Satterlee party	12
Whitmarsh	120
Whitmarsh & Co.	116, 117, 120, 121
Whitmarsh, H.	116
Whitmarsh, Hiram	113, 115
Whitney, D. Co.	118
Wigeatt Bros. & Co.	120
Wilcox, Capt. John	72
William, Bob	37
Williams, Anna	91
Williams, Christian	91
Williams, Fanny	91
Williams, George	91
Williams, Isabella	91
Williams, Robert	91
Willis and Anderson	114, 118
Willis, Thomas	115
Willis, Thos.	118
Wilson, Thomas	92
Winslow, George	20
Wizlizenus, Frederick A., M.D.	13
Wolfull, John	114, 118, 121
Woodfull, John	116
Woodward, Capt. W.	119
Woodward, W.	113
Wright, H.C.	42
Young, Brigham	22
Young, Charles E.	33
Zeeps, John	95
Zo-lah	65

www.ingramcontent.com/pod-product-compliance
Lightning Source LLC
Chambersburg PA
CBHW072143160426
43197CB00012B/2217